MODERN WITCHCRAFT

MODERN WITCHCRAFT

FACTS LEARNED FROM EXPERIENCE

BILL LOVE

FONTHILL

Fonthill Media Limited
Fonthill Media LLC
www.fonthillmedia.com
office@fonthillmedia.com

First published in 2013

British Library Cataloguing in Publication Data:
A catalogue record for this book is available from the British Library

Copyright © Toni Hughes & Jak P. Mallmann Showell, 2013

ISBN 978-1-78155-090-8

Typeset in Sabon 10/14
Printed and bound in England

CONTENTS

PART 4   LIFE AND DEATH IN WITCHCRAFT

Bill Love at home in Folkestone, Kent.

INTRODUCTION

Bill Love (that's his real name) wrote the core of this book, but died before it could be finished. Following his death, it was necessary to rewrite the first five chapters because he had left gaps and omitted some necessary explanations. As a result, this book has three authors. We have deliberately left the passages written entirely by Bill in the first person while most of those that were rewritten are in the third person.

Bill was a fighter pilot during the Second World War who studied physics at St Andrews University and later became a teacher in physical education. He had a technical mind and strong scientific understanding; he was not the sort of man to become overawed by such things as 'magic' and 'spells', but in Witchcraft he found truth and wisdom.

Bill's initiation into a Traditional Witchcraft coven with Northumbrian roots took place before Gerald Gardner brought the subject of Witchcraft to the public's attention. This is somewhat unique because Bill learned the Craft from older members who shared memories dating back to the nineteenth century. This meant that when he became High Priest, he could by-pass much of the information, processes and rituals that sprang up as a result of books written during the 1950s. He brought a more authentic pool of knowledge to the new Sacred Coven of Ceridwen in Folkestone.

The second author of this book is Toni Hughes. She has lived the Pagan way for almost twenty-five years and stood by Bill's side as his High Priestess for nearly twenty years. Together they taught and guided many initiates into the 'Old Ways' and celebrated the sabbats and the esbats with them. In 1997 Toni gained an Honours Degree in Environmental Science, which

Bill Love, one of the most open and welcoming types one could hope to meet, always remained as an unusual mixture of highly technical on the one side and deeply involved with the supernatural on the other. His study resembled a vast heap of untidiness although he always found exactly what he was looking for without having to search for it. Among his books one could find diverse subjects such as degree-level mathematics, the latest Radio Spares electronics catalogue and publications about ghost sightings.

added further to her understanding of the natural world, its energies and its processes. Following this she continued studying for a Post Compulsory Trainer/Teacher Certificate and then worked in a library before becoming a civil servant.

Toni knew Bill for over thirty years, having first met him at the Theosophical Society in the late 1970s, when Bill delivered a talk on Witchcraft. This held her interest and in the late 1980s, she attended Pagan and paranormal group discussions at Bill's house, which finally led to her initiation into the Coven of Ceridwen during the early 1990s. She readily agreed to help her mentor, friend, lover and spiritual advisor to finish the book he had started.

The third author, Jak P. Mallmann Showell, also comes from a teaching and scientific background. He met Bill in 1996 and quickly discovered that he had the same inquiring mind and dissatisfaction with the general doctrine

Bill Love, the High Priest of the Sacred
Coven of Ceridwen, wearing his brown
robe.

of modern times. Both agreed that if there is anything in the supernatural, then it will stand up to experimentation just as well as any other scientific subject. Consequently they took many opportunities to explore the natural world through experimentation.

When Bill died, Jak considered it his duty to finish the book he had been urging and helping Bill to write. Apart from this, Jak has no connection with any Witchcraft coven. He is now a full-time author, photographer and researcher specialising in modern naval history.

Hopefully readers will not object to the use of 'he' throughout much of the book; the alternative use of 'he/she' is clumsy. As far as possible we have given the names of organisations where further help might be found, but we have avoided giving web addresses because these could well be out of date by the time this book is printed. Organisations can be found via Internet search engines.

We are exceedingly grateful to the members of the Sacred Coven of Ceridwen who helped with the production of this book. The photographs of the coven were taken over a period of many days and almost all of them were set up especially to help Bill. That means that they show genuine coven activities, re-enacted for this book. All those wearing robes were genuine members of the coven when the photos were taken. The photos of the Elders are an exception in that members of the coven helped to make these pictures possible. The Sacred Coven of Ceridwen in Folkestone is currently made up of: Toni Hughes, Darren Holland, Julie Bennett, Suandra Andrews, Graham Bacon, Paula and Guy and we are exceedingly grateful for all the help and encouragement they have given. We would also like to thank Adam, Jessica, John and Lisa for their superb help, which is much appreciated.

These days, where Witchcraft is no longer banned by law, there are many people who agree that much of the secrecy is superfluous and both the Craft and outsiders considering initiation would benefit if more genuine information was made available. It would be good to expand this publication in future to a more detailed account of modern Witchcraft; the authors would be delighted to make contact with covens and hedge witches who might like to contribute to such a publication. We would be especially interested in hearing from covens that do not advertise on the Internet.

PART ONE

INTEREST
AND
INITIATION

CHAPTER 1

FIRST CONTACTS

Witchcraft, the Craft, the Old Religion or Wicca, call it what you like, has nothing to do with devil worship, satanic abuse, evil ceremonies or sacrifices. It is a way of life, of living in harmony with nature. A witch can be female or male, young and beautiful or old and wise.

It is remarkable that a technically minded Roman Catholic RAF fighter pilot, who studied physics at Scotland's oldest university and became a physical education teacher after the War, should find himself in close contact with a Traditional Witchcraft coven as early as 1942. This was outrageous and dangerous; the Witchcraft Act was not repealed until almost ten years later and the Old Religion, the pre-Christian religion of North-West Europe, was still banned. Yet, Bill Love remained firmly attached to the concept of living in harmony with nature.

In 1953 he asked to join a coven. The High Priestess who initiated him had herself been drawn to the Craft in the 1920s, and often told stories of older members with memories going back to the end of the nineteenth century. So, Bill's story has ancient roots with inherited memories from a time when everything connected to this way of life was still very much against the law. Bill did as the elders taught him and learned from the experience; in addition to this, during the 1950s, he met many of the famous people who first brought this ancient way of life to the public's attention. This provided him with unique opportunities to follow roots into spheres, which many modern practitioners of Witchcraft or Wicca can only dream about.

Jak met Bill through such extraordinary circumstances; there was a strong feeling of some hidden, yet powerful force providing the necessary guidance. It all started at a dreary lecture in Folkestone. There was a rather scrumptious buffet on one side of the room and an exceedingly long speech by the chairman on the other. Jak took advantage of the open door to explore the garden, rather than suffer the stifling heat of the stuffy gathering. Joel, a Frenchman living in England, whom Jak had briefly met before, also went out for some fresh air. The two started talking about dowsing and Joel told Jak that he had a friend interested in such things; 'You must meet him,' he said.

A few days later the phone rang, inviting Jak to a talk at Bill Love's house. This was such a striking occasion that Jak immediately agreed to attend the next meeting and after that he hardly ever missed one of Bill's Saturday evenings. The majority of people who attended these gatherings were 'free thinkers', capable of thinking outside the box without regurgitating the official lines put out by the media; many of them based their knowledge on personal experience, rather than from printed scriptures. This made the gatherings refreshing, exciting and almost addictive. A few years later, when Jak had been made redundant after the closure of the school in which he taught science, Bill and Jak met once a week, on Thursday afternoons, to explore their inner selves.

Bill Love was an extraordinary character. He was born in South Africa and often talked about how he came to live with his mother in Lydd (Kent) when he was about ten years old. He told us about his early schooldays, the secrets of Romney Marsh and the excitement of the War. Lydd was right on the front line, with many enemy aircraft flying low over the town; there were several occasions where Bill led the police to crash sites. He recalled one particularly macabre event when he and his friends found bits of what had been a pilot spread over quite a large area. This horror didn't put Bill off his dream of becoming a fighter pilot; when he was old enough he joined the Royal Air Force. Some years after the War, while studying to become a teacher at St Mary's College in London, he found himself confronted by the Old Religion once again. These days such an event would hardly spark a comment in our multicultural society, but in 1953 it was amazing. Society was different then. To understand the restrictions of those years, we need to briefly step back in time, to 1942, when Bill first came into contact with the Old Religion.

In 1942 Britain was a staunchly Christian country with the government, the media, the Church and the austerity of war dictating exactly what to think and what to do. Fringe religions were tolerated but hardly practised with any great publicity. Spiritualism, for example, had been introduced to the United Kingdom in 1853; it was condemned so heavily, especially by the Roman Catholic Church, that conversion to spiritualism actually increased in rebellion to such intolerance. There was even a Society for Psychical Research founded in the 1880s, but all of this was very much on a small scale and the majority of people would have hardly had access to these fringe organisations.

Astonishingly enough, in the middle of the Second World War in 1942, the Witchcraft Act of 1735 was still active. It was brought back to life to send a forty-five-year-old woman to prison. The facts of this case are a little blurred because the government concealed much of the proceedings; in a way, they are hardly relevant because the rumours that filtered out to the general public are more indicative of what the average person made of this most unusual event. It would appear that Helen Duncan, a practising medium, obtained psychic information about the sinking of the battleship HMS *Barham* in the Mediterranean, with a loss of at least 860 men. This came shortly after the sinking of HMS *Hood*; it was too much for the government to publish. For some reason the matter had to be kept secret for many months, but enquiries started flooding into the Admiralty as a result of Helen Duncan's séance. She was immediately arrested, tried and sent to prison for contravening the Witchcraft Act. Examples like this, of the authorities suppressing free thinking, prevented most people from becoming involved in non-Christian activities.

Yet, while Witchcraft may have been out of bounds for ordinary people, it did provide a fertile field of study for a number of academics that were seeking to spread beyond the strict limitations of the day. Margaret Murray, a brilliant professor of Egyptology at University College (London), published two books while she was still active in the university: *The Witch Cult in Western Europe* in 1921 and *The God of the Witches* in 1931. There were other authors as well; Bill often quoted from *The Golden Bough* by Sir James George Frazer, published in 1922. Although this book is hardly known in Britain, its Russian translation had a strong following in the old Soviet Union and was even included in university reading lists over there.

Bill hardly had a powerful urge to pursue any of these 'outlandish' activities and his initial interest came about as a result of being dissatisfied with the teachings of the Church. As a student at St Andrew's University he attended many discussions; none of them were terribly serious, simply an enjoyable break away from the daily mundane study. A number of like-minded friends introduced him to people living nearby so that he could attend meetings in the homes of some who lived close to the university. It was at one of these talks that he saw a bookshelf with the volumes mentioned above; the owner was obliging enough to lend him *The God of the Witches*. Bill was most surprised when he learnt that this forbidden old religion was still being practised in the more remote areas surrounding the university. He lapped up the information with great relish, but his mind was firmly focused on the War and of making a contribution towards winning it. When his studies were interrupted by the opportunity of flying with the Royal Air Force, he grabbed it without the slightest hesitation. The downside of joining the RAF was that Bill qualified as a pilot shortly before peace broke out in Europe, meaning that his operational activities came to a sudden end because there was no longer a great demand for fighter pilots.

The RAF not only provided the opportunity of fulfilling a childhood dream of flying, but it also heightened Bill's passion for competitive games; in the end, Bill decided to become a teacher of physical education because this gave him the opportunity of flying with the RAFVR (Royal Air Force Voluntary Reserve) at weekends and indulging in sport for the rest of the week. Being a Roman Catholic, Bill was attracted to St Mary's College (Strawberry Hill, Richmond, Greater London) because it had an excellent reputation for high academic standards as well as brilliant sport facilities. When he got there, Bill found that the majority of his year's intake was made up of ex-service personnel, some with considerable experience. Despite their maturity, all students had to attend chapel twice a day as well as Mass on Sundays. Sundays were never the easiest because a good number of students stayed out late the night before. On one particular occasion Bill was brought to his senses by a most astonishing sermon. He couldn't believe his ears. Here was a Roman Catholic priest talking to his congregation as if he was reading from Margaret Murray's *The God of the Witches*. Despite his extreme tiredness, Bill was enthralled and afterwards congratulated Father Michael on his splendid performance. As a result he was invited to other private discussion meetings. There, Bill found something he could neither grasp nor let go. It penetrated far into his subconscious and made him want to dive deeper into the mysteries of life. Rather than being put off by this questioning grown-up student (Bill was twenty-eight years old) Father Michael was obliging enough to suggest that Bill might like to meet some of his friends outside the college. So, with a Roman Catholic priest as pillion, Bill rode his Golden Flash motorcycle to the Epping Forest in Essex.

This page: Flight Lieutenant Bill Love became a fighter pilot and saw some action shortly before the end of the Second World War.

Vivian of Hereford

4/9/46—30/10/46.

F/L's Taylor   Webster, D.F.M.   F/O's Wright   Yates
F/L's Kenworthy   Love   Wells   S/L. Skellon   F/L's Wright   May   F/O. Russell

Above: Going to teachers' training college shortly after the War was totally different to the rigidity of military life. General conditions and food were better; there was more freedom to deal with frivolities and one could indulge in many different activities. It was like taking the lid off a boiling pot. Everybody was keen to get out, to explore the world and to find new horizons. This is the only photograph among Bill's collection showing the joyous side of college life, marked most distinctively by the typical college scarves.

Left: Bill Love chose St Mary's College at Strawberry Hill because it was renowned for high academic standards with excellent sport facilities. Sport was important to him. He represented the RAF in inter services games at Wimbledon and came close to many air force sporting records.

It may have been some ten years after that first encounter with Witchcraft at St Andrew's University, but the gap between Witchcraft and the establishment was still cavernous. The two might have been on different planets. Virtually every public performance of anything in Britain either started or finished with the national anthem, where the entire audience stood to attention. In cinemas people were known to make a rush for the doors at the end before this started, but there was also a high proportion that remained standing once the music had started. The Church also played an important part by penetrating into many aspects of everyday life. Schools always started everyday with an act of Christian worship and youth organisations were targeted by the clergy. There seemed to be no escape for youngsters. Bill Love was frustrated by these powerful Christian antics and was searching for a more satisfying explanation of the meaning of life. Although this is quite understandable these days, the steps taken by Bill were enormous, dangerous and most unusual. The average human being was prepared to put up with the idiosyncrasies of the Church by ignoring them for much of the time and standing to attention when the national anthem demanded it. Bill was different.

The Epping Forest had an air of mystique about it. It was one of the last remnants of an ancient royal hunting area; evidence suggests that the forest dates back as far as the early Stone Age. The area may have been administered by the City of London, but this authority also looked after several other commons around the edge of the capital and in those days it was far beyond daily commuter traffic. Motorways hadn't been built yet and roads through the forest were lonely and remote; there were more platforms for holding large churns awaiting the milk lorry than signposts.

Finding the way to Chipping Ongar, some ten miles beyond the forest, would have been difficult, even for an ex-fighter pilot. This was deepest rural Essex, where one was more likely to meet a herd of cows, horse-drawn vehicles or a motley collection of old farm tractors than ordinary cars. The warm smoggy London air laced with strong petrol fumes gave way to a noticeable cooler and sharper feeling in the lungs as Bill rode into the forest.

Father Michael's friends welcomed Bill into their discussions. They told him that this Old Religion didn't have a handbook or rulebook like the Bible. There were no impossible stories one was expected to believe, no communal songbook, no prayer book, no strangely clothed men who acted as an official link between man and God. In fact, according to them, there were hardly any rules at all. You could do exactly what you liked, as long as you didn't hurt anyone or anything This respect for life went as far as looking after those 'pests' which Christian gardeners killed with great relish. In fact, there was no need to kill or hurt anything at all. The Old Religion was concerned with creating the right balance and it was thought best to do that out in the open, where man-made walls did not insulate from natural forces. Natural Force was itself a little-known concept; it had much more appeal to Bill, a technically minded person, than the stuffy doctrine thrown at him previously. In fact, much of what Father Michael's friends were saying was more practical than anything officialdom had ever taught him in the past. They even talked openly about sex and fertility, saying that this was a vital part of the natural cycle and nature would come to a grinding halt if it didn't work properly. For many people, particularly Christian gardeners, fertility was something taken care of by adding the right John Innes compost; discussion didn't go much deeper than that. What Father Michael's friends were saying sounded most plausible, down to earth and attractive. Bill wanted to explore further.

But Bill felt like he had arrived at an obstacle that he couldn't pass; on the other side he saw only a wild maze. He knew for certain that he did not want to follow the doctrine of the Church, which had ruled much of his early life, but going along the path of the Old Religion was not the easiest of choices either. Bill saw himself as being in front of a locked gate. First he needed help in opening it and then he had to find a way through that maze. Father Michael's friends told him that any locked gate would remain open once he had passed through it; there was nothing stopping him from turning round and going back the way he had come. There was no contract to sign, no long lists of rules to obey, no subscriptions to pay and no unreasonable promises to make. Bill developed a strong curiosity to join a group practising this Old Religion; he wanted to penetrate further into the natural world.

Bill never clarified the relationship between Father Michael and his friends, Ray and Sheila, who lived in that comfortable house in Chipping Ongar with their pleasantly wooded garden. Father Michael must have known that there was a coven practicing the Old Religion there, although it was unlikely that he visited the house very often. After all, it took the best part of a day to travel between St Mary's College in Strawberry Hill and Chipping Ongar on public transport in those days. It was often said, especially during the days of the persecution, that priests attended Mass during the day and the Sabbat at night. So, Bill suspected that Father Michael was more deeply involved than he let on. The word Sabbat is missing in many dictionaries and must not be confused with Sabbath, the seventh day of the week as a day of rest. Sabbat means a secret meeting of witches at night.

Despite the long journey, the ride to Chipping Ongar was more than worthwhile. Ray and Sheila's house exuded a calming peace; the pressures of everyday life were noticeably absent. It was always warm and welcoming; those who attended discussions were 'free thinkers' with a strong tolerance for other people's views. One immediately felt at home.

Bill had been going to Chipping Ongar for some time, with and without Father Michael, when Sheila gave a fascinating talk about the Old Religion. It had been mentioned in the past, but never in such profound detail; Bill felt convinced that this was a field that he must explore. He asked whether there were any opportunities of joining such a group. Sheila told him that she was the High Priestess of the Sacred Coven of Ceridwen and the only way for him to join the coven was by asking her directly. A man had to ask the High Priestess and a woman the High Priest. There was no way that anyone would ever be invited to join a coven. That decision had to come from the applicant, without prompting from anyone else. There and then, without further consideration, Bill asked to join the coven. Surprisingly enough, it wasn't a terribly difficult step to take.

CHAPTER 2

JOINING THE COVEN

Once Bill had asked to join the coven, Sheila, the High Priestess of the Sacred Coven of Ceridwen, took him aside to explain what he had to do. First, she pointed out that the initiation would be like a re-birth, where Bill would be expected to appear in front of the entire the coven without any clothing. Initiation was always in the nude or skyclad as it is often called. This, in itself was a major step; only a few months earlier Bill had been severely reprimanded by his commanding officer in the RAF for not wearing regulation gloves on a relatively hot summer's day. People didn't appear in public without the proper clothes, even when swimming and on beaches. The proper form of dress was definitely part of daily life and uniforms were considered to be very important. A wardrobe stand with a tall mirror was a standard piece of furniture in most houses; no one would leave without being properly dressed and one could be sure that neighbours would comment if they saw you even adjust your clothing as you walked out into the street. The idea of carrying a drink or eating food outside was just not done. There was a mode of behaviour that everyone was expected to follow.

Sheila also outlined the promises he would have to make at the initiation and what Bill would be expected to learn. He would have to study and become proficient with various methods of divination, natural seasonal cycles, with the cosmic cycles and with more specific subjects such as the use of plants and so forth. At a much later stage he would be expected to partake in the Great Rite, a ceremony involving ritual sex. None of these presented Bill with any great problems and he saw Sheila's outline as being nothing more than an extension of his early life in the wilds of South Africa, and later among the mysterious natural marshland around Lydd.

There was no immediate response from having asked to join the coven and several months passed without a word from Chipping Ongar or from anyone vaguely connected with the coven. At times Bill felt deflated as if it had all been nothing more than an illusion, until one day he was summoned to appear before the elders. Sheila had warned him that this was likely to happen; the elders were to judge whether he would be a positive member of the group. As Bill rode towards Epping Forest on his Golden Flash motorcycle, he was not sure what the evening was going to have in store for him, but he was feeling excited.

It was late and dark when he arrived. He was immediately blindfolded and Sheila led him into a car. Half an hour's drive seemed like an eternity and he had no idea where he had been taken when the vehicle stopped. Unable to see, Bill used his other senses to guess that they had briefly passed though a house and must, once again, be standing in the open air. Music he had never heard before, what might these days be classified as 'New Age', and a hint of incense provided a comforting feeling. Despite being blindfolded, he had a strong sense that everything was going to be alright and that Sheila was going to protect him from any nasty surprises, so he was quite happy to step forwards with her holding his arm.

They stopped again. Bill heard three distinct knocks on something that resonated a little and he guessed that this was a backdoor to the garden. The deep voice of the Keeper asked clearly, 'Who goes there?'

'It is I, Sheila, High Priestess of the Sacred Coven of Ceridwen.'

'What is your purpose?' asked the deep voice.

'I seek counsel with the Elders.'

Bill remembered standing there for a while before the same deep voice said, 'The Elders grant you counsel and bid you to enter.'

When the blindfold was removed, Bill noticed he was standing by a backdoor, facing an empty garden. They were surrounded by high walls, bushes and trees. There was hardly any light other than a few candles and the small crescent of the moon. Yet, the empty darkness was neither scary nor oppressive and Bill had no qualms about venturing further; Sheila's presence provided a strong confidence that nothing untoward was likely to happen. Before him appeared a brown-hooded figure.

Holding a bell in one hand, the Keeper took a few steps towards Bill. Nobody spoke and Bill could only stare in astonishment, almost as if that music and incense, still drifting through the open air, had somehow

The guard standing over some of the Elders of the Sacred Coven of Ceridwen, with the keeper wearing a brown instead of a white gown. They keep their faces covered all the time and only the High Priest and High Priestess know the identity of the Elders.

anesthetised his senses. He had no way of knowing whether this was a man or woman. The face was covered with a big hood; the figure might have been a tailor's dummy had it not moved on its own accord. At the ringing of a bell, seven white-robed figures appeared as if from nowhere, but in fact, they were stepping out from behind thick bushes. Again no one spoke as the white clad figures with hoods over their faces stepped into a horseshoe around Bill and Sheila. There also appeared a horned figure with its face covered.

There were good reasons for this secrecy. The Elders never attend coven activities and remain unknown to its members because there always was the danger of interference by outside authorities. In the past, members were imprisoned, tortured and burned by the Christian Church. So, with the Elders unknown to the coven, there was never a way for the authorities to destroy the entire coven. The Elders would remain within the community to rekindle any flames extinguished by the official Inquisition. Persecution is still a problem to this day and later chapters will provide a deeper insight into some incendiary events of recent years.

Once the Elders had formed a semi-circle around Bill and Sheila, she addressed the group: 'Elders of Ceridwen, I bring before you Bill, child of

This page: The members of Bill's coven wear gowns while other covens dispense with them and go sky clad. During the early days gowns couldn't be purchased and therefore needed to be hand made. The members of the Sacred Coven of Ceridwen still make their own gowns.

the Goddess, who seeks initiation into our sacred coven. I beg you to show your blessing in the ancient way of the Craft.'

A bell was rung once more and Bill watched how the first figure dropped an acorn into a bowl. Each time the bell rang an Elder would or would not drop his acorn into the same bowl. All of the Elders had met Bill during earlier meetings, although he was never given any indication as to who might be a member. So, there was no need for any of them to speak. Their minds had been made up long before this most dramatic ceremonial meeting.

Bill received an overwhelming majority to which Sheila said, 'The Elders have given their blessing to your initiation into the Sacred Coven of Ceridwen.'

Then she turned to the Elders and said, 'I give you my word, this child will be good and true to the ways of the Goddess and of our Craft. Blessed Be.'

Following this, without further ado or ceremony, Bill was blindfolded again and driven back to where he had left his motorbike, to return to college. Before leaving, Sheila told him that he would be called for initiation during the next few weeks.

Initiation should be held during the waxing moon or, if possible, at full moon. The moon has the added advantage of an open-air night-time ritual by providing the necessary light, without having to add too much artificial illumination. At Bill's initiation he was taken to an upstairs room and told to take off all his clothes. The circle was opened without him and then the Handmaiden came to blindfold him and to escort him down the stairs into a candlelit room.

Bill was waiting at the north-east of the circle when Sheila's distinct voice rang out, 'Thou who standeth on the threshold of this sacred circle hast though good reason to enter?'

Bill replied, 'I have two passwords, perfect love and perfect trust.'

'All who have such are doubly welcome. I give thee a third with which to pass through this door.'

She took Bill's hand and kissed him full on the lips before guiding Bill anti-clockwise (known as deosil) around the circle and at the same time spinning him in the opposite direction (known as widdershins) until he was standing in front of the altar at the south of the circle, but with his blindfold still in position, he had no idea where he was. Incidentally, this is one of the few times that a witch moves around the circle in an anti-clockwise direction. Following this, Sheila performed the five-fold kiss before taking Bill through an oath of allegiance and proclaiming him an initiate of the Sacred Coven of Ceridwen.

The five-fold kiss can be performed silently or with words of explanation, depending on the circumstances, but usually consists of: kissing the feet which have brought the person to the place of contact; the knees so that he or she can kneel by the sacred altar; the penis or the vulva because without those the person wouldn't be there at all; the chest because in a male it helped to form the strength and the breasts of the female because they provide the first food for any offspring; and the lips because those speak the sacred names.

Following this, a Lincoln green robe was hung around Bill and fastened with a brown belt to signify his initiation into the element of earth. Only then was his blindfold removed so that Sheila could introduce him to the other hooded members standing around the circle. They kept their faces covered until the new initiate had made the promise to maintain secrecy. They lifted their hoods as Bill was introduced to them. Surprisingly to Bill, he already knew everybody present, having met them at earlier gatherings, without knowing that some of them were members of the coven.

Bill's initiation included that oath of secrecy and for more than half a century he kept to this oath. When I first met him in 1996 he was still reticent when talking about coven activities and hardly mentioned any details. In fact, he hardly ever mentioned the coven. However, things changed around this time; on several occasions he became highly agitated about events reported by the media. Yet, although he condemned things, he was never irritated enough to reveal details he had learned under the oath of secrecy. That oath was conceived at a time when the Old Religion was still banned and therefore there were good reasons to maintain a high level of secrecy. Now that Old Religion is accepted as a legal practice, Bill feels it his duty to stand up for the truth when his religion is smeared with misinformation, abused by the media or when charlatans exploit gullible people in its name. He felt justified in revealing much of the original teachings of the Old Religion because he considered the false teachings of misinformed, self-acclaimed witches to be even more harmful than attacks by the media.

Bill began to write down what he knew of the Old Religion. His first draft was full of editorial notes concerning aspects that were difficult to explain on paper but which demonstrated the depth of his understanding; with considerable prodding, a great deal of persuasion and some mild blackmail, Bill was persuaded to continue with the second version of his manuscript.

We do not know whether any other members of the Chipping Ongar coven moved away to continue practicing the Craft in other parts of the country, but in the late 1980s, Bill formed a new branch of this coven in Kent, where he was then living. Later members of that new Sacred Coven of Ceridwen urged him to continue writing and they helped in creating some the images for this book. The coven fully appreciated the importance of recording the facts and practices for posterity. Neither Bill nor the coven had any qualms about breaking that oath of secrecy to prevent the commercialisation of the Old Religion and the false practices of charlatans.

1953, when Bill was initiated, was a dynamic time. The austerity created by the War slowly gave way to the freedom espoused in the Hippie movement of the early 1960s. While Bill was working through the five degrees of Witchcraft, he was also following up leads provided by other members of the Chipping Ongar coven. Bill was led on profound avenues of mystery and intrigue, and he relished the opportunities they presented.

PART TWO

THE
OLD RELIGION
AND ITS
MODERN VARIANTS

CHAPTER 3

SPREADING OUT: WITCHCRAFT IN 1955

Bill was eagerly working through the various degrees of Witchcraft and had reached the second rung when the secretive world he was studying suddenly flooded into mainstream media. He knew that there was a coven near St Andrews University in Scotland, he had got to know another one in Sussex and he guessed that there must be a few more dotted around, but he didn't know where they were. Then, without prior warning, Gerald Gardner's book, *Witchcraft Today*, burst upon the scene.

The fact that Witchcraft was essentially the practice of living in harmony with nature was hardly mentioned. The media feasted upon out-dated medieval connotations. Gardner was immediately referred to as the Chief Witch and his activities were equated with black magic, devil worship and any other evil activities journalists could think of.

It was not only the tabloid press that started barking and biting; other witches emerged from the woodwork to condemn *Witchcraft Today*. Bill was surprised and enthralled by the fuss the book had caused; it proved that the Old Religion was far more widespread than he had imagined. He decided to go to Gerald Gardner's flat in Holland Park in London and meet him.

Gardner was born in 1884, so he was around seventy years old in 1955 when Bill first met him. Bill was surprised to see that despite their totally different ages and upbringings, they seemed to speak the same language. He discovered that *Witchcraft Today* did not reflect Gardner's true beliefs; considerable modifications had been made to appease friends who had helped him write it.

Bill described Gardner as warm and generous, a person who always seemed to have time for people who called on him. His wife, Donna, provided tea and biscuits. Time just stood still there. Gardner was eager to pass on information but he was also a good listener and would encourage visitors to talk about their experiences. The feeling of comfort and tranquillity was very much the same as that which Bill had experienced in that farmhouse near St Andrew's University and at the covenstead in Chipping Ongar. Having read *Witchcraft Today*, Bill was eager to ask the author why his book was suggesting something so different to what Bill had experienced. Bill pointed out that during their first conversations Gardner himself said that his initiation into a New Forest coven had been similar to Bill's experiences. So, why did he change direction?

Gardner explained how he and his wife moved out of London shortly before the War to live in Highcliffe, a small town to the east of Bournemouth on the Hampshire–Dorset border. The ancient New Forest, with wild ponies, huge trees and enchanting habitats, was a few miles to the north. What exactly happened down there is still open to conjecture, and anyone researching Gardner's fascinating life will quickly become entangled in contradictions, mysteries and loose ends. But the time that Bill spent with Gerald Gardner helped him to obtain a deep insight. He was told that the New Forest coven avoided publicity and the members were fiercely against having their activities published in a book.

It is important to add that during discussions with Gardner, Bill discovered that the coven he had been initiated into differed markedly from that which Gerald was advocating for his covens in his writings. But Gardner appeared to have considerable knowledge of the rites and practices of the coven that Bill belonged to. From information gleaned from Gardner, Bill formed the opinion that the New Forest coven was more akin to Bill's coven in their rites than to the system that Gardner was now promoting. Bill asked Gardner why this was and he replied that the New Forest coven was very traditional and shunned publicity, and that they were particularly averse to any revelation concerning the fact that they initiated through five degrees.

This put Gardner into a deep predicament. How could he write a book about the Old Religion and leave out its main core? Somehow, and we are not exactly sure how and why, he eventually agreed to describe only three degrees. Bill always found it strange that these three degrees were adopted by many new covens, despite having no roots within Witchcraft doctrine. His argument was that the five degrees were based on five elements: earth,

Above and below: Gerald Gardner was initiated into a New Forest coven. This magnificent area of old woodland still provides a deep core of mystique and wonder, although during those early days, before cars were common, the entire area was incredibly remote with many rare plants, animals and weird secrets lurking among the lushness of the huge forest.

water, air, fire, which were governed by spirit; therefore why should anyone study just a fraction of what was available? Again, these days we are left in a quandary and no one will probably ever get to the bottom of Gardner's thinking or the influences that made him tread this path.

It is often suggested that Doreen Valiente, a former High Priestess of Gardner's coven, influenced the concept of three degrees; after all, there are three phases of the moon, (maid, mother and crone), and there is a harmonious relationship between Witchcraft and the moon. Aleister Crowley, author of a number of books on magic and the occult, has also been mentioned as the originator of the concept of three degrees. He is also considered to be the author of the *Book of Shadows*, a document containing rituals and methods of initiation for the degrees. In fact, Ivar McKay, an antiques dealer and Freemason, suggested the concept of three degrees to Gardner and, of course, this reflects the three well-known degrees of Freemasonry: Entered Apprentice, Fellow Craft and Master Mason. They can be considered 'well known' because there are a further thirty degrees, a fact unknown to many Freemasons. It is highly likely that, as many researchers have said, Gardner 'borrowed' a great deal of information from Freemasons, whose development must have run along parallel lines to that of Witchcraft. The two must have connected in earlier years, when a good number of masons could well have been involved in Witchcraft. However, Bill decided that the concept of the three degrees has no significance in the Old Religion; it was simply born out of expediency.

Gardner had spent much his early life in mystical places of the Far East where he had many opportunities of studying 'native witch doctors' and 'natural magic'. Although such subjects are easily ridiculed, even these days, anyone searching far enough will quickly find that there is more than one sees at first glance. Some of these weird practices not only work, but they work exceedingly well. This is where Gardner and Bill had common ground; neither of them believed anything just because it had been written down. If any magic was true, then it would stand up to experiment and one could handle it in exactly the same way one might deal with any other 'biological' phenomena: design an experiment and an effective control. Yet, devising that experiment in the first place was not always easy, bearing in mind that one was dealing with invisible forces that could fade faster than the lights in a cinema.

Bill has often mentioned that Gardner met Ivar McKay, the head of The Church of the Ancient Dawn, who also lived in Kensington and practiced

Qabalistic magic. Bill stated that it was McKay, not Aleister Crowley, who helped Gardner with the Qabalistic influence in his writing of the *Book of Shadows*. The Qabalah, with a variety of different accepted spellings, means from mouth to ear and is the basis of some old 'keys' for interpreting the hidden meanings in texts like those in the Old Testament. Bill said that that system of practical magic was developed from abstruse explanations and carried out by western lodges and temples, but none of this has any place in the Old Religion, which came from northern Europe rather than from the core old Jewish world. None of this helped Bill. Rather than providing a fulfilling guide to help him make progress with his journey of personal discovery, he was frustrated by the loose ends and the contradictions of *Witchcraft Today*.

Gerald Gardner suggested Bill might make more progress if he was to meet Margaret Murray, the author of the books mentioned earlier. She was already 92, but her brain was still working to full capacity; Bill enjoyed three years of guidance from this highly respected authority. It will be remembered that Margaret Murray was Professor of Egyptology at University College in London and despite her age she maintained a room in or close to the university, so meetings were easy. Her chief apprehension was that 'the Old Religion would not continue unadulterated into perpetuity' (Bill's words). She was concerned that Gardner's book *Witchcraft Today* would result in the real meaning being twisted so far that original doctrines would be distorted beyond recognition and eventually lost forever. She stated that Gardner's book was likely to result in many covens springing up in all areas without any of the founders having been properly trained in the Craft. Bill agreed that Gardner had now created an easy bandwagon for weirdoes to jump on and it was going to become increasingly more difficult to distinguish the genuine practitioners from the charlatans.

Working in London, Bill had easy access to other sources of information and there were two of these: The Atlantis Bookshop off Bloomsbury Way and the Cosmo Coffee Bar in Finchley Road. The Atlantis bookshop is still there at 49 Museum Street, a hundred yards or so from the British Museum. Its colour and book titles have changed over the years, but its atmosphere and general contents are very much the same as they were more than half a century ago. It is the sort of place where you can pop in just because you happen to be passing and then realise many hours later that you have forgotten the real reason for coming to that part of London. There is no urgency or any distractions and it is all too easy to get lost among the masses

These pages: The Atlantis Bookshop in Museum Street by the British Museum has changed considerably over the years but still maintains its close roots to the occult, witchcraft and similar subjects. It still is the sort of place where time stands still or doesn't even seem to exist, and one can find a vast number of unusual publications not available elsewhere. Unfortunately the other important early witchcraft centre, the Cosmo Coffee Bar at Swiss Cottage, has long disappeared.

of fascinating volumes. Bill described it as follows: 'the large window in the Atlantis Bookshop was packed so full of books, posters and paintings that it was impossible to see the inside of the shop. The glazed top half of the green-painted door to the left of the window presented a similar problem due to the abundance of cards advertising tarot readers, spiritual healers, meditation groups and a plethora of other activities which would now be broadly termed *New Age*. The door allowed the faint aroma of incense to percolate to the street and the soft Eastern music seemed to beckon. Once inside, the atmosphere was conducive to browsing through the multitude of books on comparative religion, philosophy and the occult. It wasn't easy to get into a conversation with the proprietor, Michael Houghton, known in some quarters as Michael Juste. He was a little man, with a mop of white hair, who seemed to be incessantly typing as he sat behind the counter. Michael was capable of getting extremely annoyed over the most trivial event but the way to his heart, even after he had told you to get out, was to take him a coffee and a cream doughnut from the Italian café next door.

The notice board inside the Atlantis Bookshop played an important role, especially during early years when witchcraft was still prohibited in the United Kingdom.

He was magically powerful and headed The Great White Lodge that was dedicated to healing and helping those who had got out of their depth in the occult.'

In 1949 Michael Houghton also published Gerald Gardner's book *High Magic Aid* and it was his assistant, Florence Caine, who introduced Bill to the Cosmo Coffee Bar at 4-6 Northway Parade, Finchley Road. Florence was better known as Jet because she was always dashing about and couldn't seem to remain anywhere for any length of time. Coffee bar is perhaps the wrong term because the modern coffee houses hardly existed in what was then a predominately tea-orientated country, but restaurant and café would also not really describe the Cosmo. This part of the Finchley Road was developed shortly before the War as main arterial road running from London to the north and the Cosmo was just a few steps from Swiss Cottage Underground station. During the day it served as resting place and filling station for people visiting this local shopping area and at night, when the shops were closed, it was frequented by members of occult groups, by writers and journalists who were delving into such subjects. Among these people were Idries Shah, the Sufi writer, John Symonds, author of *The Beast*

666, Gerald Gardner and members of his coven including Jack Bracelin, the High Priest and author of the book *Gerald Gardner: Witch*.

Jack Bracelin, a retired Palestinian police officer, owned the Five Acres Sun Club at Bricket Wood near Watford, the home of the first Gardnerian coven. It was in the Cosmo that Bill introduced Jack to Rosemary Ellis, a philosophy student and ballet teacher, who later became his wife. Rosemary was a Roman Catholic ex-convent school girl and Jack surprised many by agreeing to marry her in a Roman Catholic Church. Afterwards they took part in hand fasting at the covenstead.

Margaret Murray's predictions that Gardner's book *Witchcraft Today* would result in conflict rather than provide a catalyst for smooth development came true at about the same time as Bill first explored the Atlantis bookshop and the Cosmo. 'It was in 1955,' Bill said, 'that I met Gerald Gardner amid the turmoil of a generally hostile press and open animosity from the High Priest of another coven based at Charlwood, not far from where Gatwick airport is now. Charles Cardell was claiming that his coven practised authentic Witchcraft and that Gerald Gardner and all his witches were charlatans.

'Charles Cardell later advertised his Dumblecott Magick Productions regularly in both *Fate* and *Prediction*, the two major occult magazines of the period. He produced a range of cold castings with occult significance and various creams and balms "secretly made where two streams meet". Profits were "for the finding of the Water City". It must be said that the craftsmanship of the products was exceedingly good and no animal or chemical ingredients were used in the creams and balms, but Cardell was a publicity seeker and quickly got his coven into the national press, complete with photographs taken in the woods near his home. He adopted the name 'Rex Nemorensis' (King of the Wood). This was taken from the title bestowed upon any runaway slave who could slay the guardian priest.

'Cardell saw Gardner as his chief adversary and it is fair to say that he was particularly jealous of the importance attached to the secrecy of the initiation rites of Gardnerian Witchcraft, which were, of course, jealously guarded by the original Gardnerians. As Gardnerian covens began to spring up in various parts of the country, the bickering, intelligence and counter-intelligence between these two rival covens continued and Cardell never missed a chance to impress the Bricket Wood coven with his powers. Bill well remembered the time when Jack Bracelin entered the Cosmo in great panic, brandishing a lengthy letter from Charles Cardell. The letter detailed the names and movements of the complete Bricket Wood coven for a period of one week. Obviously a very powerful magic had been at work to obtain all this information. The truth was far simpler; apparently, as was discovered later, he had employed private detectives but initially these disclosures did have the desired effect, even on a retired Palestine police officer.'

The final blow fell in June 1964 when, four months after Gerald Gardner's death, the back, outside full cover of *Fate Magazine* carried this advertisement:

> The Secret is Out!
> Modern Witchcraft Revealed.
> Complete Witchcraft Rituals as Taught and Practised
> by Gerald Brosseau Gardner Witch
> Presented by Rex Nemorensis.

It was unfortunate that, just as Margaret Murray had foreseen, publication of *Witchcraft Today* was swiftly followed by an upsurge of Kings of the Witches, Witch Queens (neither title has any credibility), hereditary witches and witches who were Traditional, Hereditary, Gardnerian and Alexandrian simultaneously. Photographs began to appear, particularly in the Sunday tabloids, invariably showing someone in ornate robes, standing in a double circle bearing what were supposedly 'magic' words.

Witchcraft became a bandwagon to jump on. These 'ancient' occult groups all appeared after the publication of Gardner's book. Bill often asked the simple question of where had they been before the publication of *Witchcraft Today* and why didn't they seek publicity immediately after the repeal of the Witchcraft Act in 1951? The obvious answer has got to be that the majority of the 'witches' who were now bathing in limelight didn't know anything about Witchcraft until they had read it in Gardner's book. Older, pre-war books had now been out of print for more than ten years and were then exceedingly rare. It is highly unlikely that the majority of people would have seen them. Some of these older books might have been kept in some specialised institutions but it is unlikely that the local authorities of the time would have added such volumes to their public libraries.

According to Bill, another up and coming witch, who was later to be known as 'King of the Witches' was, at about this time, trying to obtain admission to a Gardnerian coven. However, Jack Bracelin was highly

The Book or the *Book of Shadows*
with a cover decorated so that it looks
almost like a cake.

suspicious of this new candidate and he didn't succeeded in becoming a
Gardnerian. Unperturbed, Alex Sanders, who claimed to be a hereditary
witch having been initiated by his grandmother as a child, started his own
brand of Witchcraft. Amid a blaze of publicity, *Alex Sanders – King of the
Witches* was published in 1969. Alex and his wife Maxine were seen and
heard on television and radio, and many articles referring to them appeared
in the press.

In fact, according to Bill's research, Alex Sanders cannot have been initiated
as he claimed; records in Somerset House indicate that his grandmother
had died before he was born. Nevertheless, Alexandrian Witchcraft had
become a challenge to the Gardnerian sect. The truth is that there is very
little difference between the two and in Janet and Stewart Farrar's book
The Witches Way it is suggested that Alex Sanders somehow managed to get
hold of a copy of Gerald Gardner's *Book of Shadows* and formed his rituals
from this. By the time Alex Sanders came on the scene it was very easy to
get hold of a copy of the *Book of Shadows*. As has been mentioned, it was
advertised by Charles Cardell on the back cover of the June 1964 edition of
Fate magazine, four months after Gardner's death, and cost 20 shillings.

Personal computers, email and the Internet were still things of the future in those days; those who sought to tread the path of Witchcraft needed zest and stamina to find their way. But where did they have to seek? Clues were to be found in *Prediction* and *Fate* magazines, the two leading occult publications in those days, and the Theosophical Society notice boards and announcements posted in the Atlantis Bookshop and Watkins Bookshop in London's Cecil Court. For those who could decipher the clues, it meant that they were assured of meeting genuine practitioners of the Craft on a face-to-face basis and, from the point of view of the Craft, it eliminated time wasters, thrill seekers and the like at an early stage rather than after a lengthy period of fruitless communication.

With the advent of email and the internet, it has become much more time consuming to sort the true seeker from the sensationalist. There are many covens inviting people to join: there are even more individuals looking for contacts. It is quite easy to spot those who have never really grasped the true meaning of Witchcraft. One such person, who advertised on the Internet, wanted to find a coven whose members were under twenty years old, to teach her everything about Witchcraft. How could someone just out of their teens teach something which takes a lifetime to learn? Quite apart from that, the Old Religion and Christianity do not have age barriers.

Another coven, with a lengthy website, clearly states that the disabled are not accepted. This is about as anti-Wiccan as anyone could imagine, but that same coven initiates on a waning moon and draws blood as part of the initiation ceremony: a practice which, in many Gardnerian covens and certainly in Traditional covens, would be considered unethical, unnecessary and dangerous. This kind of ceremony belongs more to the province of the sorcerer and shows a total lack of knowledge of the very fundamentals of Witchcraft. Good covens can be found today, as they could be in earlier times, but the web makes the undesirable covens much easier to access.

A misleading concept, which seems to have crept into websites, is to describe Gardnerian and Alexandrian covens as Traditional. Janet Farrar and Gavin Bone also fell into this error in their first Question and Answer column in *Pentacle* magazine. This is totally wrong. Traditional covens are those that existed before the birth of modern Witchcraft in 1954 and there is a glaring fundamental difference in the teaching: Traditionals are initiated through five degrees. Bill never understood why the New Forest coven was so averse to Gerald referring to five degrees, which are linked to the Aristotelian Elements. After all, this follows from the basic concept that the Universe consists of four elements (earth, water, air and fire) governed by spirit and represented symbolically by the pentagram. The Gardnerians of those times certainly knew of the existence of Traditional covens, which are still 'out there' today, but are difficult to find because they do not seek publicity.

There has been too much meddling with the Old Religion since it first appeared in the public domain following the publication of *Witchcraft Today*; Margaret Murray's fears have been vindicated. It is to be regretted that the Old Religion has evolved into a considerable commercial enterprise since the days when Gerald Gardner, in an effort to publicise something that he saw as spiritually and socially uplifting, invented a botched variety because of a warning from the New Forest coven.

The magazines and the web are full of advertisements offering nice little packages like spell kits, some very special because they are hand made! Spells, of course, cannot be learned from a kit. Many advertisements display a photograph of a 'witch', wearing a flamboyant silk dress and masses of jewellery, who can solve problems relating to love, health, money, curses and other issues for anyone willing to pay for a consultation on a premium rate line. You can, if you wish, obtain a worthless diploma in anything from Creating Talismans to Energy Healing for Animals for £20-£100 or more. Before smoking was prohibited in public places, one also found such people at psychic fairs where one paid to get in and then a bit more if one wished to take advantage of healing services on offer. Yet on looking closely one could see some of these healers surrounded by a heap of weird paraphernalia and they often had a saucer serving as ashtray for a large pile of cigarette ends. These days such people have to nip outside for a quick drag and therefore do not leave such distasteful evidence on their display table, but the same characters are still around. How can they help anyone if they can't control their own lives without anaesthetising it with smoke, alcohol or drugs?

The concept of a witch name is another facet that has crept into this bizarre scene. This ridiculous practice is also unsound magically, where it is essential to use the name by which you have always been known and addressed. A 'witch', who is trying to impress a crowd, is far more likely to have been a humble housewife in a previous incarnation than a temple dancer or a Spanish whore, as one well-known witch, who has appeared on television and written books, claims to have been. It has been demonstrated scientifically that nothing seems to penetrate deeper into the subconscious than the name used by a mother to call her baby, so why break away from this naturally strong bond?

Why do some 'witches' find it necessary to wear a robe when they attend a function such as the so-called Witchfest? Are they trying to say, 'Look, I really am a witch?' This kind of exhibitionism does not do the Craft any good. A robe is a sacred garment and should only be worn for ritual purposes. No Traditional witch would ever dream of abusing a robe in this fashion. There are many other examples of 'playing at Witchcraft', a situation that has become all too prevalent in modern Wicca.

Trendy phrases and terms such as *Beltane Bash* and *Witchfest*, and attempts to play to the gallery do nothing to enhance the true concept of the Old Religion. Spell kits, astrology kits and rune kits, all neatly wrapped in plastic, and complete with full instructions, smack of the supermarket culture and bear no relationship to the Old Religion which is committed to embracing and experiencing nature in all her aspects.

Traditional Witchcraft has its own mystique, which is more than sufficient to whet the appetite of the true seeker and provide the encouragement to embark on the exciting and rewarding journey along the Old Path.

Postscript

Earlier in this chapter Bill mentioned Florence or Jet, as she was known, who worked in the Atlantis bookshop in London during the mid-1950s. I (Jak) met her accidentally under the strangest circumstances, while carrying out some interview research in Lindfield (Sussex) for the German U-boat Museum. On the way to my interview I dropped a friend off at a house nearby. She was visiting an old acquaintance there. That evening, when I came back to pick up my friend, I entered the house and met a most stunning lady. She was obviously not in the best of health, but she still got out of bed to talk to me. She looked incredibly attractive; somehow she had an air of brilliance and majesty and I was even more spellbound when she started speaking. Sadly the conversation lasted only for a short while, but later I discovered that this striking person was none other than Bill's old friend, Florence Cane (Jet).

CHAPTER 4

ROOTS, HURDLES AND SUPPRESSION

By the time Bill met Gerald Gardner, he had worked his way up to the second degree in the coven and therefore had a reasonable knowledge of what one might call the Craft's language. The big problem with this was that many of those who knew this in the past couldn't read or write and those who spent their time studying the languages of the day were guided away from such practices as Witchcraft. Early Freemasons overcame this problem of not being by masters of the trade passing on special codes and rituals to their understudies. Thus any employer could easily check the level a new applicant had reached. One should be able to assume that a good number of early masons also dabbled in natural forces and therefore it is quite likely that Masonic teachings hold good clues as to how Witchcraft has developed in the past.

Even though many witches were illiterate, they still recorded noteworthy events. The problem is finding where information has been stored and then interpreting the evidence. As Bill's knowledge improved, so did his ability to decipher some of the information around him; he pieced it together, like a jigsaw puzzle, to see the overall picture. The average person would look upon many of the old symbols as mere decorations, without understanding their significance or even recognising them as Witchcraft marks. Bill had that sort of inquiring mind that drove him into far-off places, searching for snippets that might help him understand the Craft. The rest of this chapter is based entirely on Bill's research, on the talks he gave at his Saturday meetings and on the manuscript of his book.

It is not difficult to work out that the need for food and the strong urge to reproduce must have been at the very centre of early life. Since Witchcraft

Above, left and right: Bill sitting on the stairs of his home during one of his Saturday evening meetings. A dozen or so people usually fitted into his small living room and at times he managed to accommodate as many as 25-30, although then it became a bit of a squash. These meetings usually started with a talk followed by a discussion on a wide variety of subjects from Jehovah's Witnesses to UFOs. The vast majority of the people who attended were 'free thinkers', capable of thinking outside the box (or laterally) instead of regurgitating the official lines put out by the media. Many based their knowledge on personal experience rather than from reading books. This made Bill's meeting most refreshing and attractive.

originated in northern latitudes, this old way of living in harmony with nature must have been subject to severe seasonal variation, even after mankind had settled down to take up farming instead of being full-time hunter-gatherers. This seasonal variation, with temperatures on the continent ranging from -20°C in the winter to well above 30°C in summer was at the basis of the Craft. It is not difficult to find evidence that knowledge of what is going to happen, long before it actually happens, was an important part of the struggle to survive. So, for early man, it was essential to ensure that the natural balance was in his favour, and that he was well prepared for the expected hard times ahead.

We do know from modern remote tribes that their preparation for a group hunt includes special dances and rituals to get into the mind of the animals they are going to look for. It would seem that this was also the case in prehistoric Europe. There are cave paintings of hunting men with one of them dressed as the horned animal being hunted. This suggested to Bill that this might have been part of a ceremonial procedure; if the clothing was

Above, right and next page: It is easy to determine the seasons, each with its characteristic features, but in the olden days it was also necessary to work out when each season would finish and the next one was due to start. Following natural cycles was not easy without modern weather forecasts and calendars.

for protection or being used as tool, then all the hunters would have worn it. In addition to old cave paintings, there is other evidence to suggest that the concept of a horned god was widespread throughout Europe's northern latitudes.

Dr Anne Ross, author of *Pagan Celtic Britain*, produced a vast collection of pictures showing inscriptions on pottery, stones and metal objects depicting horned figures. It would seem that there are two of these: one with antlers and the other looking like a bull. In both cases it is often fairly obvious that the animals are males rather than females with udders. It is strange that these days we equate Vikings with horns on their helmets, although there is hardly any evidence that these were ever fitted to protective headgear.

It would seem that the worship of horned gods continued for several centuries throughout the Roman occupation and lasted until long after the spread of Christianity. As society became more complex and more people specialised in skilled trades enabling them to live in stable communities, it became important to control the lives of each individual inside it; what better way than using the doctrines of the Christian Church? The basic message was easy to understand: each individual was working for God and therefore he gave much of his labours to the high officials who had the special power

Early man's horned god was made into the devil by Christian churches and often represented as a hideous creature, as seen here in Canterbury (Kent).

Witches suffered from a bad press, and were represented by the Church as hideous evil characters. No one was ever told that they were people who wanted to live in harmony with nature rather than obey the rules and regulations put out by big religious organisations.

to communicate with this one god. By giving away much of their labour, the ordinary people were certain to secure a better position in their 'afterlife'. In the Old Religion each individual has a direct line to the natural gods and there was no need to support a hierarchy of 'better people'. Such a free and easy lifestyle had to be repressed if the control mechanism was going to function effectively for the benefit of the rulers. It was not difficult for the early Christians to convert the old horned god into an evil devil and thus change people's thinking.

The turning point in the attitude of the Christian church towards the Old Religion seem to have come towards the end of the fifteenth century when Pope Innocent VIII issued his *Summis Desiderantes Affectibus*. This condemned Witchcraft, as it was then called, and friars were appointed with the necessary power to suppress what was being looked upon as a religious uprising centred in what is now Germany. The result was a publication called *Malleus Maleficarum* or the *Hammer of the Witches* and this provided the authority for judges, magistrates, priests and other officials to carry out a far-reaching Inquisition. Now government authorities were able to torture innocent people to extract confessions, and then put them to death. As a result the Old Religion was pushed to the verge of extinction.

This barbaric persecution lasted for parts of the sixteenth and seventeenth centuries and, since it allowed them to confiscate property and wealth from the witches they condemned, it made the authorities exceedingly rich. Some of these unfortunate victims were given a fair trial by the Church, based on the knowledge that a tightly bound body of an innocent person would sink when thrown into water and only guilty people would float. It is incredible that the institutions of Government and Church agreed to such vile treatment. The scale of the torture and execution was considerable. The county sessions in the small town of Bury St Edmunds (Suffolk) tried some 200 people during one session of the Inquisition. Bearing in mind that the population in those days was well below 3,000, this represented a considerable proportion of the total. It would seem that in some places witches were burned at the rate of one a week and old etchings suggest that this took place during public meetings, such as market days, rather than in secret. That would suggest the majority of people would have witnessed the enormous suffering the leaders of the Christian Church were inflicting upon their hard-pressed followers.

Things simmered down a little during the seventeenth century. It would be good to think that this came about as a result of a realisation that mankind wasn't going to get terribly far under such ferocious persecution by the Christian church, but in reality the change in attitude was due to outside influences. The Thirty Years War started in 1618 between German Catholics and Protestants and its influence spread rapidly throughout Europe, creating serious economic and political turmoil. Denmark, Sweden and France became involved, resulting in a dramatic deterioration of living conditions throughout central Europe. Much of the country between Calais in France and Holland was under Spanish rule and the so-called United Provinces ruled the north of Holland. This fighting and upheaval resulted in refugees crossing the North Sea to seek safer havens along the British coast. The Church's attention was turned away from persecuting old women. Very few men were burned during the Inquisition; the highest proportion was made up of married women.

Bill recorded that the last execution for Witchcraft took place in 1684, when Alice Molland was hanged in Exeter (Devon). Witchcraft must have occupied the minds of the authorities for some years to come because as late as 1735 the government passed the Official Witchcraft Act, which remained on the statute books until 1951, when it was replaced by the Fraudulent Mediums Act. The last person to be persecuted under the Witchcraft Act of 1735 appears to be Helen Duncan in 1942, who was mentioned earlier regarding the sinking of the battleship HMS *Barham* by the German submarine U331 under Kapitänleutnant Hans-Diedrich Freiherr von Tiesenhausen.

The sad thing is that the abolition of the Witchcraft Act and the creation of the Fraudulent Mediums Act of 1951 did not put an end to the persecution of people wanting to practise the Old Religion. Bill followed a number of the more recent witch hunt cases in the national newspapers and on television. Modern persecutions appear to have been sparked off by Doreen Irvine's book *From Witchcraft to Christ*, published in 1972. She claimed to have been the High Priestess of a satanic group in the United Kingdom and explained how demons helped her to float near the ceiling of rooms, but no one ever witnessed any of these events and none of them were ever proved. Another book, *Michelle Remembers*, by Michelle Smith with the help of the psychiatrist Dr Lawrence Pazder, was published in 1980 and triggered a surge in allegations of satanic cruelty. According to the newspapers of the time, parts of America erupted with so many stories of child abuse that international consultants were brought in to help with the investigations. Yet, despite all the media hype, it would seem that the charges were either abandoned for lack of evidence or discarded by juries. Bearing in mind that this satanic abuse involved something approaching a thousand people, the devil must have been highly successful in covering all the morbid evidence.

Of course, if satanic abuse excites people in America, then there have to be similar goings-on in the United Kingdom; it was not long before the media over here started bursting with breathtaking headlines. Bill reported that the first case was in Cheshire in 1987, and this was followed by incidents in Rochdale and Nottingham and near his old coven ground in the Epping Forest. The fascinating point about these incidents is that they became more bizarre as time went on. The climax came in 1989, when there were some police raids on several families. Nine children were woken up, abducted from their beds by the authorities and evidence of satanic activity was seized from their homes. This included a model aircraft identified as a satanic cross, a priest's cloak that was considered completely out of place in the house of a sixty-eight-year-old Presbyterian minister, some academic hoods as worn with university gowns and some nativity masks. The investigations continued for several weeks while the taxpayers funded the bonanza, paid for keeping the terrified children in care and ensured the payment of the investigators' salaries. In the end no real evidence was found and no one could connect any of the collected items with devil worship. With the lives of several families in tatters and both adults and children highly traumatised, the case was dropped and the evidence returned.

Virginia Bottomley, the Health Secretary at the time, appointed the anthropologist Professor Jean La Fontaine to compile a report into satanic abuse and this was published by HMSO in 1994. The conclusions were that 'evangelical Christians had encouraged and influenced the concepts of satanic abuse and both psychologists and social workers had engineered the hysteria'. The result of all this upheaval was that ignorant thrill seekers of society now knew for certain that the devil was definitely living among them, but that he was difficult to detect because he always went around in disguise. It was obvious to them that anyone with any connection to horns or even someone liking such items must have a strong connection to satanic abuse, and such people had to be hunted down. Everybody seemed keen on jumping onto the bandwagon and even a member of parliament brought the matter up in the House of Commons, saying some fifty children were killed each year in the United Kingdom in satanic rituals. But no one ever produced any evidence of these ill doings. It appeared that any story relating to child abuse with the devil's involvement was given the highest priority and some of them were pursued by officialdom even after such cases collapsed due to the lack of evidence.

There was an incident where a mother appeared at a school parents' evening wearing nothing more than sandals and a see-through slip with see-through knickers underneath, leaving absolutely nothing to the imagination. A few days later she accused a teacher of kissing her daughter. The teacher was immediately suspended and a special police team was brought in to deal with this serious offence of child abuse. These investigations were abandoned again because neither the mother nor the girl could say when this happened, where it happened or how the kissing had taken place. Both of them agreed that the accused teacher had never been alone with the girl, but neither of them could remember who else was present at the time when the kissing had taken place. Yet, despite this, the teacher remained suspended while county education officers, unqualified for such delicate investigations, carried out another full enquiry. This was considered necessary because the mother was known to drink too much cheap alcohol and was often tipsy, so it could have been that she had disguised the poignant smell of her drinking while talking to the police, who then missed some vital evidence. The teacher was called for interview to be tormented into making a confession, which he refused to do. Then another week or so passed while the education officers took legal advice before demanding that the teacher be returned immediately to work. The fact that he had now been severely traumatised was not taken into account. All forms of child abuse are abhorrent and perpetrators of any such cruel action, whether against children or adults should be severely dealt with. It is just such a pity that this often appears not to happen and rapists and murderers are released early from jail to repeat their morbid activities against other unsuspecting victims.

The sad point about such cases is that many ordinary people who wish to live in harmony with nature are persecuted merely because they seek an understanding of natural cycles. Bill said that with all this persecution during the sixteenth and seventeenth centuries and again more recently, it is difficult to see how it would be possible to claim unbroken lineage from earliest times to the present day. The interesting point is that no sensible practitioner of Traditional Witchcraft has ever made that claim. Bill and a large number of other researchers have said that it seems likely from archaeological evidence that Traditional Witchcraft is close to a religion that was practised during the Celtic Period, when a spirit force was worshipped through the Horned God and the Great Earth Mother.

It should also be emphasised here that children do not take part in coven activities. When youngsters are present during discussion meetings or at outings, the conversation is adjusted to take their presence into account. (Bill's coven never initiated anyone under the age of eighteen.)

PART THREE

THE ESSENCE
OF THE
OLD RELIGION

CHAPTER 5

TRADITIONAL WITCHCRAFT

Traditional Witchcraft is the Old Religion or the Old Way of Life, based on some later elements of the pre-Christian religion of North West Europe while Gardnerian and Alexandrian Wicca (or Witchcraft) are based on the post-1954 teachings of two men, although some members are happy also to adopt older ideas. Essentially, Traditional Witchcraft is a way of living in harmony with nature and honouring the Goddess and the God; therefore it is hardly a 'belief' in the way of most other religions. Our ancient ancestors must have lived exceedingly close to the natural elements. Traditional Witchcraft is something everyone can experience; it has never been a purely ritualistic activity carried out only at special meetings in designated places. It is a way of life that offers a path through *everyday* life, not just for special occasions laid aside for worship.

The abundance of books and websites have inevitably led to confusion and doubt concerning the fundamental aims of Witchcraft and this may have been exacerbated when Gerald Gardner deemed it necessary to institute three degrees of initiation instead of the five of the Old Religion. However, the aims have never deviated in the practice of what has now become known as Traditional Witchcraft. Before the word Wicca became widespread in the mid twentieth century, it was known simply as Witchcraft, the Craft or possibly a multitude of local names.

Traditional Witchcraft embraces teachings, which have been handed down by word of mouth over the years and practised in small groups known as covens; this is where modern practitioners are faced with complicated problems. In addition to natural misunderstandings, which are bound to occur among any group in any situation no matter how hard the participants try to avoid duplicity, there were also many deliberate attempts to falsify details. A confession by Isobel Gowdie at her trial in 1662, saying that there were thirteen members in each coven, has often been accepted as the authoritative. However, many of these confessions were obtained under torture or the threat of it and the trials were usually conducted in ecclesiastical courts. Even if it was a court of civil law, the officials would have been staunch Christians and it was therefore easy for the prosecution to submit that witches were diabolically empowered and blasphemous.

Born of the Earth Mother and sired by the Sky Father, those who gathered in the groves and greenwoods to pay homage and show reverence to the Great Mother, the giver of all life, were happy and joyous people. At the four great feast days, which represented turning points in the Wheel of the Year, they showed their thanks to Mother Earth for the plentiful harvests which provided succour during the long winter, and they ended the celebrations with feasting, dancing and games which often had a sexual connotation; a reminder of the importance of fertility for survival. These four great celebrations and feast days became known as the Greater Sabbats and later, with the influx of astronomical knowledge from Greece and Egypt, the solstices and equinoxes also became feast days, later to be known as the Lesser Sabbats.

The Christian Church has equated this activity with the worship of evil and human sacrifice, but no evidence of this has been found. Villainy is not a modern invention; it is not surprising that archaeologists, digging in the cesspits of bygone ages should find evidence of foul deeds. But evidence of peaceful societies is also found. The shores of the Baltic provide some enriching sources of information. Some Iron Age Vikings lived there in houses built on long poles in shallow water, deep enough to prevent anyone from wanting to attack by wading through, but also too shallow for sea going boats to get close. The people there didn't need a weekly dustcart; rubbish was just dropped into the water. Added to this were more valuable items, possibly at times when the places came under attack. Archaeologists excavating such sites have produced a harmonious picture of a well-structured society; no evidence at all of any sacrifices was found. In fact, judging from bones found in the mud below the settlement, it would appear that the early Vikings didn't even go hunting and obtained almost all their meat from domesticated animals.

The Great Mother is a primordial image, an image that has always existed. This image exists within the human psyche and finds outward expression in the rituals, mythology and art of early mankind, and in dreams, fantasies and creative work in modern times. In analytical psychology, these primordial images are known as archetypal, inner images and are present in the human psyche where they function with astounding regularity. The effects of these archetypes can be experienced in consciousness and can affect the personality. It is possible that some people might reject or repress these basic thoughts, but that does not mean that such impulses do not stir from the subconscious.

The image of the Great Mother is formed gradually in a growing baby and is later strengthened with reminders of her. These reminders are usually nature symbols such as oddly shaped trees, pools of water, animals or stones. The primordial archetypes of images combine both positive and negative attributes. To early mankind, the godhead was one and embodied the attributes of good and evil, friendly and unfriendly. It was only as consciousness developed that these attributes developed into the Good Goddess and the Bad Goddess, which were different beings.

Over a long period of time these archetypal images took form and were reproduced as art, sculpture and simple decoration on everyday objects. Dr Carl Gustav Jung, the Swiss founder of analytical psychology, discovered that the archetypes were rooted in the collective unconscious and manifest in the 'mythological motifs' that appear among all peoples at all times. The archetype has a profound influence on the human psyche and is therefore bound to be a directing force in religious thought. According to Jung, 'Myth is the primordial language natural to these psychic processes, and no intellectual formulation comes anywhere near the richness and expressiveness of mythical imagery'. When the inner images are projected into the conscious mind they become 'real', as if they are being experienced. The figures of the gods and goddesses can therefore become real.

One of the oldest of images is the vessel, which appears as a bowl, goblet, chalice, cornucopia, grail and the receptacle of the alchemists. The body is also universally experienced as a vessel but, to early man, the body of a woman was a special vessel because it could produce offspring. She was the 'giver of life' when a man planted his seed inside her and she then provided nourishment, warmth and protection. She was the mother but these were not the only qualities of the mother. There was also a mysterious and unseen side: she was rhythmic and cyclic and, like the moon, also had a dark side. Earth too was a mother; all life was brought forth from her. She was the mother of all vegetation on which all other life ultimately depended. She

The majority of people hardly ever look at the sky, cannot understand the meaning of clouds and have no knowledge about the importance of the moon; yet this is one of the most powerful influences on natural cycles.

was the Great Earth Mother. This is the archetypal concept on which all fertility rituals and many myths are based.

We of the Old Path do not suggest for a moment that we are practising rites that, despite the cruel persecution meted out by Christian fundamentalists, particularly between the fifteenth and seventeenth centuries, have survived unscathed. However, the Old Religion, as it is practised today, is based on a number of folk beliefs that have survived, often as myth, from the distant past. Many of these have been Christianised, particularly those that were deeply entrenched in rituals. Imbolg, celebrated on 1 February, was a pre-Christian Feast of Light in which fiery torches were paraded through settlements. However, it was Christianised as Candlemas Day on 2 February when the candles used in the churches are blessed. This is why many authors, including the Farrars, place the Imbolg sabbat on 2 February, but academic sources and Celtic authorities, like Anne Ross, clearly place Imbolg on 1 February. Easter is the festival commemorating the resurrection of Christ but before that it was the festival of the Teutonic goddess Eostre, which took place at the Spring Equinox.

Easter is held on the Sunday after the first full moon following the Spring Equinox. How very Pagan! Eggs have always been symbols of reincarnation and the continuity of life and were used at the great festival of Beltane and at the Spring Equinox to celebrate the revival of nature. Hard-boiled eggs, dyed in bright colours and often elaborately decorated, were used in divination and in games such as egg rolling. The early Christians converted them into symbols of Christ's resurrection and they were taken to churches to be blessed without any thought of their Pagan heritage.

Right: Easter has become one of big moneymaking festivals of our age where millions of people buy over-priced every-day products because marketing campaigns urge them to do so. One wonders how many actually know the origins of this most humble festival and how many still celebrate it the way it used to be done.

Below: A ceremony symbolising the three aspects of the moon. The colours of the gowns represent the waxing moon (white on the left), the full moon (red in the middle) and the waning moon (black).

All religion can be divided into two fundamental aspects: beliefs and rites. Beliefs express the nature of all sacred things. In Traditional Witchcraft, as well as the goddesses and gods, these include the wonders of nature: the fragrance of the wildwood; the song of the wind caressing the willows where two streams meet; the blossom of the blue cornflower embracing the bees in their unrelenting search for nectar; the haunting shriek of the barn owl as it glides silently and spectre-like beneath the crescent moon; the eerie glow of will-o'-the-wisp flitting across the marshland pond; and the huge orange harvest moon hanging low in the autumn sky. It is among such scenes, far from urban falsity, where Traditionals find the goddesses and gods of old.

Emile Durkheim, the French sociologist, says in his book *The Elementary Forms of the Religious Life* that, 'rites are a manner of acting which take rise in the midst of assembled groups and which are destined to excite, maintain or recreate certain mental states in these groups'. The mental states so created enable the participants of the rites to gain access to their unconscious mind and thus to the astral, or what Jung called the 'collective unconscious'. The rites, it is true to say, are kept guarded, but there is a reason for this. Covens have, over perhaps many years, developed a system of ritual based on a goddess or god. Such groups have built up a thought form or a collective group mind, which forms a collective entity, an egregore. Once this thought form has been established it is possible for members of that group and those that work with the same system to enter into a sympathetic relationship with the astral body and thus have access to inner realities and solutions to everyday problems.

This concept can be exceedingly difficult to grasp, but it has been studied by leading scientists and has not been concocted by weirdoes. What is even more interesting is that biologists studying wild animals have described the same concept. There was a case where one wild chimpanzee gained some superiority within his group as a result of beating an empty tin can. Soon afterwards other biologists, studying chimpanzees a long way away, started reporting similar incidents among their troop. One wonders whether this was a case of information travelling through what Jung called the *collective unconscious*?

We cannot begin to understand God, the divine power or whatever one wants to call it, which we believe is present in everything that exists everywhere at the same time, so mankind has turned to worshipping this power through a god on our own physical plane. In doing so, they have often humanised the force. In the Old Religion the Horned God came to represent virility, death and the winter months, and the Goddess, fertility, rebirth and the summer months. The Horned God is the personification of nature, the God of Hunting, and the God of Death, but as the symbolic essence of the fertility-creating phallus he is also the Lord of Life. The Goddess is the Great Mother, Mother Nature. We reject a patriarchal concept of one supreme detached god ruling over everything and we endeavour to live in harmonious relationship with nature. We recognise that nature is cyclic such as night and day, the phases of the moon and the seasons. That is why we celebrate the great feast days, the Greater and Lesser Sabbats, which are the very expression of the tides of nature.

The rites partaken by Traditionals are based on the recognition of the goddesses and gods and on the cyclic nature of life. Although Traditionals celebrate the eight festivals of the year, particular importance is attached to the Greater Sabbats: Beltane (1 May), Lughnasadh (1 August), Samhain (1 November) and Imbolc (1 February).

The Sabbats are also festive occasions and begin on the eve of these dates. After the sacred circle has been appropriately closed, there follows time for feasting and games. During the celebratory rites, the atmosphere becomes electric; Traditionals would never deny that the games that follow can naturally tend to become rather raunchy, but this can also occur in the excitement pertaining in any party, especially if it is accompanied with a good flow of alcohol. The problem with using drugs and alcohol is that the person taking them relinquishes control of body and mind. Similar results can be achieved by using the mind alone and thus it is possible to explore 'peculiar happenings' with the advantage that one can also learn how to control these influences and switch them off instantly when they are no longer required. One does not have to wait for the drug to wear off.

Sex plays an important role in the Old Religion. It is not simply an expression of love; there is also the psychological aspect of the release of pent up energy and repressed complexes and the very important magical aspect, which will be mentioned in greater detail in another chapter. The Old Religion has never seen sex between consenting partners as a sin; it is considered to be a perfectly natural act, which alleviates the stress that does so much damage to mental and physical health and constitutes a barrier to the spiritual path. The games played at the Sabbats help to release the shackles of convention, inhibition and guilt that prevent so many from leading a full and happy life. They also 'earth' or neutralise the tremendous unused energy that has been liberated during the ritual.

Those seeking to join a Traditional coven must positively ask to do so; males ask the High Priestess and females ask the High Priest. Following this, the Elders and members of the coven make it their business to meet the prospective member without the latter revealing that they are themselves initiates. During a coven meeting, a vote is taken and, if successful, the candidate is later presented before the Elders in a ceremony that is profound and mystical and inculcates the sense of responsibility and commitment necessary for membership of the coven. If the Elders approve, initiation follows on the night of a sabbat or at some other time during a waxing moon.

The Elders are part of a highly secret inner circle who have shown a great commitment to the principles of the Old Religion. Only the High Priestess and the High Priest know their identity, which is never revealed to any other initiate, hence they are always hooded when new candidates, seeking initiation, appear before them. Although they are not members of the coven, they may celebrate the festivals in their own way. Some Gardnerian and Alexandrian covens also appoint a body of Elders from among their members; in such covens, the Elders are known to the coven members. The reason for this secrecy has been explained on page 24.

A coven consists of a High Priestess, High Priest, Hand Maiden and a number of priestesses and priests. The High Priest is the magician and it is he who imparts the universal power into the High Priestess in a ritual known as 'Drawing Down the Moon', which takes place before the opening of the Circle. Once this has been done, it is the High Priestess who directs all the activities in the Circle; its opening and closing, any healing and the form of any ritual. In the Circle, the High Priestess has unlimited power and it is essential that there should be the greatest rapport between her and the High Priest.

The Hand Maiden has an important role in the running of a coven; she is the assistant to both the High Priestess and the High Priest and, in the absence of the High Priestess, it is she who takes on that role. Consequently, there also needs to be a very close rapport between the Hand Maiden and the High Priest. In order to have the capacity to absorb and assimilate the power drawn down by the High Priest, the Hand Maiden, like the High Priestess, should be at least a third degree witch who will have received the Great Rite and is thus a channel for the power drawn down. Every member of a coven, whatever stage they have reached, must willingly accept the authority of the High Priestess and High Priest and also the Hand Maiden, whenever she is standing in for the High Priestess.

Above and below: Crystal ball divination. Staring into a crystal ball helps people to enter a state of deep relaxation by anesthetising the optic nerve and thus allowing other forms of stimulation, especially feelings, to play a greater role than when making use of the conscious part of the brain. Similar effects can be created by using hypnosis.

There are five degrees of initiation into the four elements and spirit. The elements are taken in order of increasing ethereality: earth, water, air and fire coordinated by spirit. After initiation, the beginner is taught the practical rudiments of herbalism, divination, healing and other arts, which are all essential for leading a full and happy life. There is also an important esoteric aspect in which the influences that emanate from those who have received initiation through the elements gradually attune the new member to higher and higher vibrations, and thus to the realms of magic.

Initiation into the Old Religion is always in the nude; it is an initiation or rebirth into a new way of life in which the newcomer will find himself or herself among friends who, while not living in each other's pockets, are always available to help in times of need. A coven functions as a clan or tribe and many members find themselves closer to other coven members than to their own kinsfolk. This is the way a coven should feel in accordance with their passwords into the circle during initiation: perfect love and perfect trust. Witches of the Old Religion, whenever they meet a witch of the opposite sex, greet each other with a hug and a kiss full on the lips and the words 'blessed be'. Witches of the same sex normally give a hug or a handshake before saying 'blessed be'.

There is a marked difference between Traditional Witchcraft and that of Gardnerian Witchcraft and its derivatives, which is exemplified in the first-degree initiation. In Gardnerian Witchcraft, the Qabalistic Cross forms part of the ritual for the Opening of the Circle and since this comes from an ancient system of Jewish mysticism, it has no place in the Old Religion.

With the candidate for admission standing at the Door of the Circle, the initiator says 'Thou who standest on the threshold between the pleasant world of men and the dread domains of the Lords of the Outer Spaces, hast thou the courage to make the assay?'

The postulant replies saying, 'I have two passwords, perfect love and perfect trust.'

The initiator then says, 'All who have such are doubly welcome. I give thee a third to pass thee through this dread door.'

Use of the words *dread domains of the Lords of the Outer Spaces* and *to pass thee through this dread door* is in deep contrast to the opening ritual used in Traditional Witchcraft.

Traditional Witchcraft sees the Circle as a sacred and peaceful environment, protected by the 'Mighty Ones', which are, of course, the Great Archangels of the magical Lodge and the Temple. Hence, in Traditional Witchcraft, the

Above and below: The formal part of witchcraft ceremonies is usually followed by a rest, games or frivolities, and the party atmosphere may often continue for longer than the serious part of the meeting. Members of a coven regard each other as brothers and sisters and therefore have no qualms in getting close to each other.

Haithabu, a reconstructed Iron Age settlement on the shores of the River Schlei in North Germany, the sort of place where serious witchcraft emerged as an essential part of life, rather than a religion, long before the Christian Church found its way into these remote regions.

initiator says, 'Thou who standest on the threshold of this Sacred Circle, hast thou good reason to enter?'

The candidate replies as in Gardnerian Witchcraft but in Gardnerian Witchcraft, the postulant is pushed through the Door into the Circle whereas, in Traditional Witchcraft, the postulant is invited into the Circle with open arms. The basis of the Gardnerian ritual probably comes from the Traditional coven into which Gerald Gardner was initiated but it has been altered to give the flavour of a book of spells and invocation, which is totally out of keeping with the Old Religion.

Those of us who tread the Old Path always respect the religious beliefs of others but we do not abide by their rules. We worship the same creator because there can only be one but we worship through the intermediary of a goddess and a god which we can understand and which also emphasise the importance of the balance of the female and male principles. This balance is of the utmost importance in the Old Religion; female members of the coven should be in constant contact with the High Priest and male members with the High Priestess. This is also clear from the fact that male initiates female and female initiates male. In *The Witches Way* the Farrars quote occasions when witches can initiate members of their own gender. 'A woman may initiate her own daughter, or a man his own son because they are part of themselves'. This is never acceptable in the Old Religion.

The term Traditional Witchcraft came about to differentiate it from the Witchcraft practices advocated by Gerald Gardner in *Witchcraft Today*. Unfortunately, many other varieties of Witchcraft have appeared since the publication of Gardner's book and this has led to the completely false assumption that Traditional Witchcraft refers to Gardnerian Witchcraft or Alexandrian, which followed when Alex Sanders bought a copy of Gardner's *Book of Shadows* from Charles Cardell, as is explained in an earlier chapter. Traditional Witchcraft should be known as the Old Religion which, before *Witchcraft Today* was published, was often referred to as the Craft.

Those who aspire to initiation by way of the Craft would do well to seek a coven of the Old Religion. It will not be easy to find one, and anyone who does will discover that it will be even more difficult to be accepted as a candidate, but the rewards will make all the efforts worthwhile. Newcomers will find themselves among true and sincere friends; happy people who have found the Goddess and whose intuition and feeling allow them to live in true rapport with nature; true witches who live the way of the Old Religion.

CHAPTER 6

THE FIVE DEGREES

Traditional Witchcraft, the Old Religion or the Craft, has always been associated with a system of five degrees representing initiation into the five elements: earth, water, air and fire governed by spirit. It is not difficult to understand how the concept of four basic elements occurred. Early man must have formed some vague idea concerning the nature of the material world he inhabited. He could walk and run on the solid earth and wade or swim in the water that sustained him, and he felt the strong winds that often impeded his progress. He also discovered how to make fire, which protected him from the cold and allowed him to cook his food. In addition to this, there was still a mysterious something that seemed to dominate these elements and ensure regularity in nature; it controlled the seasons, night and day, the breeding periods, the fall of the leaves in autumn and the sprouting of new plants in the spring. Man found he could learn to take best advantage of the four elements of life, but the force he felt controlling these natural cycles was beyond his comprehension. There was no way at all that he could hope to control it, so it was best to enter into some kind of rapport with it, so that it would help him rather than make life more difficult. This is manifested in the concept of initiation through the elements and spirit.

The elements are generally thought of as a relic of Aristotelian cosmology from about 350 BC, but there is evidence that they were recognised in India and Egypt more than a thousand years before this. The material world was thought to consist of a uniform prime matter that manifested as the four elements. Four qualities – hot, cold, dry and moist – were associated with the four elements, each of which possessed two of these qualities. The qualities could interact and cause one substance to become another by a process of transmutation. Transmutation takes place naturally in the sun and other stars during the process of nuclear fusion, in which energy is produced as hydrogen is transmuted into the heavier helium. This occurs only at very high temperatures caused by the immense gravitational force of these bodies. Lurking over the four elements was a rather nebulous fifth, the ether or spirit that neo-Platonists referred to as the Logos, and Medieval philosophers called the Quinta Essentia.

In learned circles, particularly among the humanists during the Renaissance, a new surge of interest in Aristotelianism appeared. Alchemists were exploring a new dimension, the belief that the universal spirit could be concentrated in the Philosopher's Stone, which in addition to being able to transmute base metals into gold, could also be the maker of life. The Philosopher's Stone was formed by combining the pure seeds of gold and silver with the aid of the Hermetic Stream, a solvent used in the preparation of other substances and known also by the alchemists as heavy water or water that didn't wet the hands. In modern times heavy water refers to water in which some of the hydrogen atoms have been replaced by deuterium, an isotope of hydrogen containing a neutron, making them heavier than the normal hydrogen atoms. Heavy water has become familiar from atomic energy and the so-called hydrogen bomb.

In ordinary water, about 1 part in 4,500 is heavy water. The alchemists spent long periods distilling water and it could be wondered whether they knew something that we don't. Abu Musa Jabir, a pupil of Muhammad al-Sadiq, the Islamic 6th Imam and a great possessor of the secret sciences, was said to have produced water in which the quality 'moist' was removed by repeating the distillation some seven hundred times.

Because observations often gave it credence, most chemists accepted the four-element theory until about the middle of the eighteenth century, the time of Antoine Lavoisier, a French chemist and biologist born in 1743, who was responsible for changing people's thinking. Following this, as Frances Yates says in her *Occult Philosophy*, 'the scientific principle held in common by Christians, Muslims and Jews was a new theory of the elements. Earth, water and air now represented the three states of matter – solid, liquid and gas, and fire represented energy, the agent that brought about material change.'

The trouble with these early scientists is that although many of them came up with the most astonishing advances, they had only limited opportunities

The High Priestess of the Sacred Coven of Ceridwen asking the Mighty Ones for protection of the circle by using an athame for drawing a pentagram in the air. Bill, the High Priest, watches from the right.

of communicating their discoveries to the outside world. Far too often the Church objected to any ideas contradicting the scriptures and punished those who published their thoughts. In addition to this, there were only very few with the necessary education to understand what these people of vision were saying.

The elements are represented in the most sacred symbol of the Old Religion, the pentagram; a symbol generally associated with magic and the occult and, quite frequently, and incorrectly, with evil. In fact, the pentagram, during the Middle Ages, was placed on doors and windows to protect homes against demons and can still be found in some country areas today. The fifth verse of the old folksong *Green grow the rushes, o* mentions this in the words 'Five is the symbol at your door'. The Hebrews associated the pentagram with the five books of the Pentateuch and Christians, during the Middle Ages, said that it represented the five wounds of Christ. Indeed, interpretation can be difficult and there is often more than one explanation.

In *The Witches Bible*, Janet and Stewart Farrar, referring to second-degree initiation, state that while American witches always use the upright pentagram, European witches 'still use the traditional inverted pentagram with the two

Above: The passing of the mead with the altar in the foreground.

Right: Julie arranging the layout of the altar.

points uppermost'. They go on to say 'although the four elements of earth, air, fire and water are now in balance, they still dominate the fifth, spirit'. It would appear that the Spirit only rules the elements after third-degree initiation. In the Old Religion, the pentagram is always displayed with the single point uppermost because the Old religion takes the view that spirit always rules all the elements and many Gardnerian covens also adopt this view.

It may be wondered why, when looking at the pentagram, the elements of air and water appear to be reversed from their orientation with respect to the altar. We always view the altar objectively and the element of air is represented to the east, which is on our right-hand side, but the pentagram is a sacred symbol that is also used subjectively; we back into it making the element of air still on our right-hand side. As we are now standing, facing the altar, the elements of air and water are correctly placed with fire to the south. Spirit is at the head and our feet are firmly planted on earth.

Two fundamental beliefs of the Old Religion are also revealed in the pentagram: everything in nature is inexorably linked and numbers have a profound influence on our lives. The pentagram has often been called the endless knot because it can be drawn without taking the pencil off the paper, which is symbolic of continuity and everything being linked. From the times of the ancient Greeks the role played by numbers in the mystery of the universe has always puzzled the mind.

Pythagoras founded a mystical philosophy based on numbers and their ratios and Plato's later view was that nature is framed upon a mathematical basis and it is in mathematics that the ultimate realities are to be found. In more recent times much attention has been focused on pattern and numerical arrangement in nature. The protrusions on a pineapple run in spirals, 8 clockwise and 13 anti-clockwise. The individual parts of the yellow centre of a daisy are arranged in such a fashion that 21 of them form a clockwise spiral and 34 of them form an anti-clockwise spiral. The numbers 8, 13, 21 and 34 are consecutive terms of part of a series of numbers which occur abundantly in nature and in which each term of the series is the sum of the preceding two terms:

0, 1, 1, 2, 3, 5, 8, 13, 21, 34, 55, 89 and so on.

This series is known as the Fibonacci series, after Leonardo Fibonacci (Leonardo of Pisa), a thirteenth-century mathematician. Two thousand years earlier, ancient Greek geometers were very interested in what they called the golden section. This was a ratio obtained when a line is divided in such a way that the ratio of the shorter section to the longer section is equal to the ratio of the longer section to the whole line.

A_____B_____C

AB/BC = BC/AC and whatever the length of the line, this ratio is always equal to 0.618034 to six significant figures. This is the golden section and successive ratios of the Fibonacci series get closer and closer to this number.

It is not known why the pentagram became such an important symbol in the Old Religion, or at what stage this occurred. Could it be that the ratio of the golden section, which is so common in nature, is deeply embedded in the unconscious? Perhaps it manifests in the symbol of the pentagram in the conscious minds of followers of the Old Religion because of their deep and sincere relationship with nature. Whatever the reason, it is an important sacred symbol signifying the four elements governed by spirit and can usually be found in a prominent position in the homes of those who travel the Old Path.

The elements must not be considered to resemble the elements of the periodic table taught in school chemistry lessons. They are a symbolic representation of fundamental qualities found in the Universe and in mankind: as above, so below. An initiatory process into any of the elements provides a new insight into the qualities of that element and this is generally followed by a change in circumstances and the emergence of new opportunities.

The element of earth, represented on the altar by the pentacle or pentagram, on which stands a bowl of earth, is concerned with life on the physical plane. Initiation into this element fosters self-sufficiency by inculcating functional, versatile and practical attributes. Water, symbolised by the chalice, is the element of the emotions and initiation into this cultivates the qualities of sensitivity, intuition, sincerity, instinct and consideration. The element of air, denoted by the wand, is concerned with the mental and communicative faculties. Initiation into this develops intensity of reasoning power and it is the first initiation in which the Great Rite is performed. Fire, denoted by the athame, is associated with energy, assertiveness, vigour and activity; it is the element of magic. Initiation into this element puts the initiate in touch with occult forces. The term occult simply means 'hidden' and, in the natural world, these forces are normally hidden from the uninitiated. Initiation into spirit occurs when the postulant is in command of all the faculties enhanced by initiation into the four elements.

Above and below: The altar is often decorated with flowers or fruit as well as the ceremonial accoutrements.

Fire, one of basic natural elements, deeply ingrained in the human subconscious, is used for variety of different purposes. It can represent death and life, both at the same time. This is the eternal flame of the war memorial in Noginsk (Russia) where it reminds present generations of the sacrifices made by their forebears in defence of their homeland.

Followers of the Old Religion subscribe to the concept that forces and images, hidden from the uninitiated, can easily be illustrated with modern three-dimensional pictures, often consisting of confusing or plain patterns. When looking at these in a special way while relaxing the eyes one sees a previously unseen 3-D image appear almost as if my magic. The uninitiated just see the pattern without the hidden image.

The elements are inhabited by forces that function at a higher vibratory rate than life on the physical plane and, consequently, they are not generally observed. They are often thought of as nature spirits but are more correctly referred to as elementals so as not to confuse them with true nature spirits such as, for example, dryads or tree spirits. Earth elementals are known as Gnomes, water elementals as Undines, air elementals as Sylphs and fire elementals as Salamanders.

Gnomes are ruled by Gob and, like other elementals, will help humans subjectively via the unconscious mind; they can be called upon to assist in any circumstances concerning material matters. They will cultivate endurance and the strength of mind to deal with financial problems and other 'down to earth' difficulties; the nuts and bolts concerned with life on the physical plane. They can be helpful and trusted allies, but if their trust is betrayed, they can cause great despair and despondency. They are abundant among rocks and in caves and deep fissures and are the guardians of treasures, precious stones and minerals.

Undines, ruled by Necksa, inhabit the element of water so, as would be expected, their presence has a considerable influence on the emotions, passion and sensuality. They are friendly towards humans and should be called upon to help in emotional issues concerning love, affection or stress. Undines are plentiful and most active in sparkling waterfalls or springs and in peaceful streams or wells. They hate and avoid stagnant pools.

Sylphs, ruled by Paralda, are beings that live in the element of air and are consequently associated with the mind. They are prolific in light mountain breezes where the air is pure. Although Sylphs tend to be aloof, they will readily respond to cries for help in matters pertaining to the mind, which they are able to influence.

Salamanders are ruled by Djin and are the elementals associated with fire. Because of their assertiveness, they are the elementals called upon in most magical work, but care has to be taken because they can affect temperament. This is one reason why a 'cool head' is essential when embarking on any magical project. Although the elementals are not generally observed, there is a method by which they can be recognised and this is taught in Traditional covens.

Salamanders' association with fire is easily explained. Theses black newt-like creatures with brilliant yellow spots hibernate in old rotting timber and when this is brought indoors for burning on the fire, they are likely to wake up and jump out. Hence the connection to fire.

It may have been noticed at the beginning of this chapter that, in the Old Religion, the elements appear in order of increasing ethereality; earth, water, air and fire, becoming more airy or spirit-like. Initiation through the degrees takes place in this order. During the process of initiation, the initiate faces an ordeal corresponding to the element. For example, second-degree initiation into the element of water may involve walking blindfold over a swaying bridge with the swirling water running beneath and splashing onto the feet and legs of the initiate. During initiation into the element of fire, the initiate hears the crackling that accompanies burning and feels the warmth wafting over the body. This, of course, is psychodrama, which 'speaks' to the unconscious mind and evokes the appropriate elemental response into the conscious mind.

It is assumed that those who seek initiation into the Old Religion have a firm commitment to make progress along the Old Path. This commitment

Above and below: Early morning ground mists are a natural feature of low-lying sandy places and can be most irritating for travellers. The ground is often hidden under a grey sheet while the sky is clearly visible. This means that path markers such as trees formed an important part of early life.

is shown by the proficiency attained in the teaching appropriate to each degree. There is no set time necessary for progress to successive degrees but some books mention a period of a year and a day. This has no foundation whatever in the Craft. The aim should always be to make progress as quickly as possible, particularly through the first and second degrees, so as to become involved in the magical aspect of the Craft. A coven full of first-degree initiates is not successful. It should never be forgotten that some learn quicker than others and quick learners should never be discouraged and slow learners should not be looked down upon.

It can never be emphasised too much that magic, which includes healing and spells, is a function of the unconscious mind and the whole of the teaching of the Old Religion is directed towards the breaking down of the endo-psychic barrier which allows a smooth and flowing interchange between the conscious and unconscious mind. This is achieved by *experiencing* certain techniques under the guidance of members of the coven who are initiates of the fourth or fifth degree and have themselves *experienced* the techniques.

While Bill has outlined some of the basic thinking for initiation into the five degrees, it must be emphasized that the lessons cannot be learned from a textbook, the same way one would study for a school examination. Right from the beginning one is confronted by feelings and these must be experienced; they cannot be learned by reading. Witchcraft has fascinated the media and many films have been made about the subject. In fact, recent books and films about Harry Potter have been the most successful ever produced. Unfortunately natural energy or natural forces are nowhere near as dramatic as the film effects and considerable skill and some training is necessary to experience them. Yet, it is not difficult to devise scientific experiments to prove that these forces exist. The problem is very much the same as climbing the Wrekin in Shropshire, one of England's mystical hills. Anyone walking up from the Forest Glen at the bottom by the old water works will soon come to a summit. Only when they reach it can they see there is another summit higher up. The same situation occurs when one reaches that summit. There is another one even higher. So, now imagine going up on a foggy day. The uninitiated could well imagine that he has reached the top without knowing that there is a good deal of exciting track still ahead of him. So, one comes to that situation Bill found himself in when he saw himself by a barrier with a maze on the other side. You can go on alone, but it is much safer and far more rewarding when accompanied by a guide who has been along that path before.

CHAPTER 7
THE WITCH'S CALENDAR

Some 12,000 years ago, dating back to Palaeolithic times, early man left a remarkable pictorial record of his activities, his prowess as a hunter and the animals he hunted. But as the population increased, hunting became inadequate for the requirements of the tribe and thus gave way to pastoralism. Pastoralism is the name given to the herding and husbandry of domesticated animals in order to provide sustenance.

It is quite evident that successful hunting or pastoral activities could not be carried out without careful observation of natural processes and the regularity with which they occurred. In other words in order to be successful it was essential to have a sound knowledge of the cyclic processes of nature. These cyclic processes were seen to be related to changes in the position of the sun. Fire, being symbolic of the sun, often featured in ceremonies. Do bear in mind that early man had neither calendars, clocks, frequent news bulletins nor weather forecasts and these cyclic processes were essential if he was going to survive as a successful farmer.

Early man's preoccupation was to control the course of nature for practical ends and he attempted this by using magic in rites and spells. Because it was essential to ensure an abundance of animals in order to provide food and clothing, many of the rites were concerned with fertility. In fact, there is evidence that there was a period in world history in which fertility and phallic rites dominated religion and this continued when pastoralism gave way to agriculture and certain rites were deemed necessary to ensure the fertility of the crops and animals.

Understanding fertility in domestic animals and humans was an essential part of early life and at a guess the average youngster of the time would have been better informed about sexual matters than his modern, highly educated counterpart. Now it forms part of the National Curriculum but in earlier times this understanding made the difference between life and death.

Because both hunting and pastoral peoples depended for their very existence on the adequate fertility of animals, it was to be expected that such peoples would be particularly interested in the breeding seasons. Two of the Greater Sabbats, 1 May and the 1 November, divide the year into two and, as Margaret Murray says in her book, *The God of the Witches*, these two divisions correspond with the opening of the two main breeding seasons for animals. These two dates, together with 1 February and 1 August were days on which important events took place regarding stock rearing and the fertility of animals. These days thus appeared as four major peaks in the Celtic ritual calendar and great festivals were held to celebrate them. The Celtic ritual calendar was related to the raising of cattle and the solstices and equinoxes played no part in the celebrations. Following later invasions, the summer and winter solstices, together with the spring and autumn equinoxes, all of which depended on the sun, also gave rise to festive occasions.

The first and most essential requirement for any human community is to be able to feed itself. Everything we eat comes directly or indirectly from the earth. This is a fact whether we eat animal or vegetable products, but when pastoralism gave way to agriculture the crops came directly from the earth so it was essential to ensure that the earth was fertile. The Earth Mother was worshipped and because the moon seemed to be able to influence the earth's fertility, the Moon Goddess was also worshipped. Moon and earth were inextricably linked.

In the above paragraphs we have the fundamental principles of the Old Religion:

1. The knowledge that nature is a cyclic process.
2. The importance of fertility for survival.
3. The realisation that earth is a living entity and that there should be a symbiotic relationship between moon and earth; a close rapport with nature.

The knowledge that nature is a cyclic process, important events recurring periodically, gives rise to a ritual calendar; the Wheel of the Year. In the course of time such a calendar becomes reinforced by folk traditions but early festivals can also become hidden when a new religion adopts or adapts a festival because it has become too well entrenched among the people. This was so essential to mankind that even the immense power of the Christian Church could not change it for its own ends; church life also had to be intertwined with these natural cycles. Yet, people intent on studying these natural cycles were still looked upon as trading with the devil.

There are four days in the Celtic calendar that persistently recur in literature and, in the Old Religion today, they are still deemed to be particularly important festivals. They are the four days known as the Greater Sabbats. These sabbats have attracted considerable attention, first by judges and investigators during the time of the Inquisition, and today by the press in their periodical outbursts on the subject of Witchcraft and devil worship, which they always confuse.

The Christian concept of the sabbat evolved during the fourteenth and fifteenth centuries at a time when suspicion, gossip or denunciation was considered sufficient to be brought before the Inquisition. The Old Religion was still deeply entrenched, particularly in remote areas, and it is said that some priests attended the Mass by day and the Sabbat by night. The new religion of Christianity was experiencing great difficulty in its attempts to replace the Old Religion and it also had to compete with Mithraism, which

Toni, the High Priestess of the Sacred Coven of Ceridwen, at an instructional meeting using a flip chart to explain the annual cycles.

had steadily grown from about 1400 BC. (Mithras was the god of light from Persian mythology, who was also worshipped by the Romans.) Clearly, for the new to survive, the good of the old had to become the bad of the new and unscrupulous followers of the Church denigrated what were, in fact, ancient religious festivals based on a knowledge of, and rapport with, nature. The two great Celtic festivals, beginning on May Eve and November Eve and continuing through the night, marked the arrival of summer and winter. These festivals, together with those beginning on August Eve and February Eve, are known as the Greater Sabbats.

The great festival of Samhain, beginning on 31 October, not only marked the arrival of winter, it was also the beginning of the Celtic year. It pre-dates the agricultural calendar because the reaping of the harvest was completed long before the festival but it does correspond to the pastoral calendar: the beginning of winter being the time when cattle were brought back from the pastures to the safety of the stalls. The festival is thus very old, dating from the time when the Celts were pastoral people. It represents, together with Beltane, a terrestrial division of the year; a division that preceded a celestial division based on the solstices and equinoxes.

From ancient times, the peasants have kindled bonfires on certain days of the year and used them to form the focal point of the festivities, dancing round them and leaping over them. Samhain was one of these ancient Celtic fire festivals and, as early as the eighth century, the Christians proclaimed fire festivals to be heathen and attempted to stop them. Yet, despite Bavaria in southern Germany being predominantly Catholic, in the mountains they still practice activities reminiscent of ancient fire festival, which now bring in masses of tourists to watch the most dramatic spectacles.

Samhain has always been a time for divination to foretell the fortunes of the coming year. Eggs are a life emblem and are believed to contain the seeds of the future, so egg divining was performed to indicate one's fortune. The procedure was to pierce the egg and catch the drops of the white in a dish of water; the shapes that formed could indicate trends for the future. Samhain was also the time when the souls of the departed were able to visit their old homes and friends and share in the good cheer that was provided, but more mischievous spirits, such as spectres, hobgoblins and the little folk, wandered around at this time as well. The fires had a ritual aspect, which was thought to rid the countryside of these impish spirits.

Many of the ancient customs associated with the Samhain festivities continued long after Christianity was established and it became expedient to change the name of the celebration to All Saints' Day or All Hallows Day, the first day of Hallowtide, a brief period of sanctity at the beginning of winter which also includes All Soul's Day. Hallowe'en is the eve of Hallowtide and the name comes from the Old English word meaning holy. The fires continued but they were then used to ward off witches and evil spirits, as were the turnip lanterns that were hung on gateposts where they could protect the house.

Games played at present day Hallowe'en parties are often taken from what were once serious divination rites. An example of this is the game to discover a future lover in which an apple is carefully peeled at midnight and the long, unbroken strip of peel is thrown over the left shoulder. The peel on the ground forms the lover's initial. Pranks play an important role in Hallowe'en celebrations and, until quite recently, Mischief Night was held on 31 October, reminiscent of the mischievous spirits that were once deemed to be abroad at Samhain. Today, in covens of the Old Religion, a suitable ritual is followed by traditional games and feasting.

Another fire festival, Imbolg, held on 1 February, was a fertility celebration traditionally associated with the lactation of the cattle and the re-appearance of vegetation following the winter's sleep. Because it was the pre-Christian Feast of Lights it was easily Christianised to Candlemas Day, which, for some reason, is held on 2 February resulting in some books giving the same date for Imbolg. Imbolg is the feast day of the ancient Celtic goddess, Bridgit, a triple moon goddess Christianised as St Bridgit. She is the goddess of healing, smith craft and poets. Bridgit, as the Triple Goddess, represents the three phases of the moon; the light of the moon is a fertilising power. The sacred fires, kindled during the Sabbat, symbolised the power of fertility, and burning during the night, they invoked the fertilising power of the moon.

The great festival of Beltane begins on the Eve of May and continues through the night to welcome the beginning of the Celtic summer. It is another fire festival and is the survival of an early pastoral celebration that marked the time when the herds were turned out to wild pasture after being driven through the fire or between two fires to increase fertility and protect them from diseases. Merrymaking and dancing round the fire, which was symbolic of the life-giving sun, was a feature of this important celebration. When the party was over, the ashes of the fire were scattered to increase the fertility of the pastures.

That the fires had a ritual significance is shown by the fact that they were originally kindled by the Druids and then, as Christianity became established, the priests took over the role of kindling and a different interpretation was put on the custom and this was used to attack witches. Sir James Frazer gives a number of examples of this in his classic work *The Golden Bough*. In Scotland, for instance, people would dance through the fire shouting, 'Fire, Fire, burn the witches'. In Germany, May Eve is known as Walpurgis Night, named after an eighth-century English nun who founded religious houses in Germany.

Lughnasadh is the feast of Lugh, a sun god who was thought of as The Shining One. This begins on the Eve of August and, like the other Greater Sabbats, continues through the night. Lugh was the inventor of all the arts and skills and was the commander of the Tuatha De Danann in Ireland. Lughnasadh, which later became Lughmass, commemorates his death. As pastoralism changed to agriculture, the Sabbat became closely associated with the first appearance of the corn and this presented a way to Christianise the festival without confrontation: the first new corn of the year, or bread made from it, was offered as thanksgiving for the harvest. The celebration was changed to Lammas, which is derived from the Anglo-Saxon Hlafmaesse, meaning loaf mass.

The Sabbat was celebrated with games, contests, marriages and the customary feast and the whole theme of the festival, even after it became

Christianised, shows once again how the people were in close rapport with nature just as present-day members of Traditional covens are.

The Lesser Sabbats are held at the equinoxes and solstices. The equinoxes occur twice a year when the sun crosses the equator and day and night are equal, giving rise to our spring and autumn. The solstices also occur twice a year when the midday sun is overhead at the northern and southern tropics; the farthest point from the equator. When the midday sun is overhead at the Tropic of Cancer, we have our Summer Solstice, and when it is overhead at the Tropic of Capricorn, it is the time for our Winter Solstice.

The Winter Solstice was regarded as the Nativity of the Sun because, at this time of the year, the days begin to lengthen and the sun increases in power. It appears that Christmas was 'borrowed' from this considerably more ancient festival when fires were kindled to celebrate the birth of the sun and Christians took part in the festivities. It was therefore expedient to transfer the Christian Nativity, which was held on 6 January, to 25 December, the Nativity of the Sun in the old calendar. Many countries, including Russia, still celebrate Christmas on 7 January.

The Anglo-Saxon name for the Winter Solstice was Yule, which is derived from the Old Norse Jol meaning a wheel. The Old English Giuli was the name of the twelfth month. Because the Winter Solstice marks the rebirth of the sun, symbolic fires were kindled; later candles served the same purpose. The Yule Log has taken the place of the outdoor fire and in many places it is customary to keep the log burning until Twelfth Night, when the ashes are collected and kept for the protection of the house.

The Yule Sabbat is a time for joy with games, plenty of candles and presents. The Yule Log should burn brightly and there should also be evergreens such as holly, ivy and mistletoe.

At the Spring Equinox the midday sun is vertically overhead at the Equator and day and night are equal. There is a balance between light and dark but light is increasing in power and will triumph at the Summer Solstice when the midday sun is overhead at the Tropic of Cancer. There is a close similarity between some of the magical customs of spring and those of Beltane because both are intended to ensure the revival of nature, which should be the theme for celebrating this Sabbat. The sun, as the giver of life that spurs the dormant vegetation into activity, is symbolised by the kindling of the fire or by a Fire Wheel, a wheel surrounded by candles and greenery.

The period at or near the Summer Solstice is known as Midsummer but Midsummer's Day is officially on 24 June and has been Christianised as the

Bill always paid particular attention to detail. The altar had to be laid out correctly and he usually insisted on having a real wood fire. Even on warm days his fire always added a comforting dimension to what was going on. People who attended Bill's meetings often remarked on the calmness and warmth in his house.

Feast of the Nativity of St John the Baptist. Midsummer festivities, held at the solstice, which is on, or near, 21 June, are very old and were celebrated with fires that were kindled to assist magically the sun that was about to wane. The fires were thought to promote fertility in mankind, herds and crops and they drove out evil. This was a time when flaming tar- barrels and burning straw wheels were rolled down hills and torchlight processions were seen.

A feature common to Midsummer festivals everywhere is the importance attached to lovers and couples who leap over the fire hand in hand or throw flowers to each other across the flames. As Frazer says, 'It is the time of the roses and of love.' In the West Country, Midsummer Eve was called the Witches Night and it was a night for divination in which eggs played an important role. Eggs were broken and the pattern they made was studied to see if any pattern formed would foretell the future.

Following the Autumn Equinox on 21 September, the sun is moving towards the Southern Tropic and, in Britain, the days are getting shorter and the nights longer; nature is slowing down for a period of rest. The harvest has been gathered in but the spirit of the corn lives on in the Corn Dolly until spring when it will once again foster and protect the next crop. Decorations for this Sabbat should include corn and its close associate, the field poppy, which is a symbol of Demeter, the corn goddess. Demeter was Romanised to Ceres who carried poppies and wheat in her hand and from whom the word cereal was derived.

This chapter on the witch's calendar is by no means an exhaustive; it is, like most of the chapters, merely an indication of activities that will be encountered by a new candidate in a Traditional coven. It must be reiterated that the Old Religion had to become a secret oral tradition and the teachings are passed 'from mouth to ear' and then experienced. Those readers who have interested themselves in magic will realise that this is in step with the esoteric teachings of Lodges and Temples. The cornerstone of the Western magical tradition is the Qabalah, which literally means 'from mouth to ear'.

CHAPTER 8

THE OLD RELIGION IN FOLKLORE AND FESTIVALS

Centuries of Christian teaching and conditioning in Britain have not killed off the Pagan gods and goddesses. They live today in folklore and custom, in archaeology and rites, in the days of the week and in superstition, and they live, and are worshipped, in the ever-increasing number of covens that are emerging in towns and country.

Present-day festivals, fairs and customs are often revivals or Christianised versions of ancient Pagan religious festivals. The two themes running through many of these celebrations are the constant conflict between opposites and the cycle of birth, life, death and rebirth. These are often portrayed in symbolic form and a god or goddess presides over, or is represented in, the festivities.

Early inhabitants of the British Isles, the Celts, Romans and the Saxons, who were brought over by the Romans as mercenary soldiers, have left a legacy of festivals, customs and their Pagan gods and goddesses. Three gods and a goddess, venerated in Anglo-Saxon Britain, have given their names to four days of the week.

Tuesday, which in old English was Tiwesdaeg, the third day of the week, is named after Tiwaz, an early Germanic war god and ancestor of Odin. Tuesday was also sacred to Mars, the Roman god of war. At a later date in the heathen period, Woden took over the function of the god of war, but Tiwaz was also associated with law and justice and was thought to be the old Sky Father.

The Saxons worshipped a sky god called Irmin whose temple and sacred wood of Irminsul, also known as the World Pillar because it upheld everything in the universe, was destroyed by Charles the Great. Irmin was a Saxon name for the sky god Tiwaz and Mars was known as Hermin. It is interesting to note that the magical colour correspondence for Mars is red, and a red horse, which was associated with Tiw, was cut into Edge Hill at Tysoe in Warwickshire. A useful practical point should perhaps be mentioned here. At Yule, the coloured balls on the tree represent the seven ancient 'planets' and the first ball to be placed on the tree should be the colour of the planetary correspondence for the particular day of the week. Hence, if Yule falls on a Tuesday, the colour of the first ball should be red. In England, Tiwaz was known as Tiw or Tig and evidence for the existence of this Pagan god can be found in many place names such as Tuesley in Surrey, Tysoe in Warwickshire and Tifield in Sussex.

Wednesday, the fourth day of the week, derives its name from the Germanic god Wodan who appeared as Woden in England and Odin in Sweden; he was the divine ancestor of most of the Anglo-Saxon kings. Both Woden and Odin rode with the Wild Hunt that, according to myth and legend, roamed the stormy skies, the hounds baying to the sound of the thunder. It was held by the Christians that these huntsmen, who streaked across the sky on their ghostly steeds, were the souls of the un-baptised, the Pagans. The Romans equated Woden with Mercury, the messenger of the gods and, in France, Wednesday is Mercredi. The magical colour correspondence for Mercury is yellow or grey.

Thunor, the Anglo-Saxon god of thunder, corresponding to the Norse god Thor, had the fifth day of the week named after him and Thursday was Thunresdaeg, the day of thunder in Old English. Like all gods of Indo-European origin, Thunor was a weather god who was worshipped by Roman soldiers as Jupiter; Thursday was the sacred day of Jupiter. The magical colour correspondence for Jupiter is purple or indigo. Thursday is Donnerstag in German, meaning Thunder Day.

The goddess Frigg, the wife of Woden, gives her name to Friday, which was known as Friesdaeg, the day of Frigg in Old English. Frigg was mother of the gods and Mother Earth and was identified with Venus, the Roman goddess of love. The magical colour correspondence for Venus is green or light blue.

The sites of long-forgotten sacred groves, gods, goddesses, holy wells and many other vestiges of the past are to be found today in place names of the British Isles. Water is perhaps the most important requirement for any settlement; villages which are not situated on a river have to obtain their

Man has probably always worshipped water and built houses close to where it pours out of the ground. These days, holy wells in the United Kingdom have been named after Christian saints, but many of these are older than Christianity. The early churches of whatever denomination were more like community centres rather than being there exclusively for worship. This incredible building stands near natural springs at Gremyatchiy Klyutch to the east of Moscow. Viktor Schauberger made the stunning discovery that drinking one litre of such natural spring water increases the weight of a person by about 1,050 g, although a litre of water should weigh only 1,000 g. He put the additional weight down to the natural energy in the water.

water supply from wells or springs. Therefore, these have been venerated from the distant past and a powerful water spirit has been considered to dwell within them. Prayer and sacrifice was offered to the water spirit and, at the times of the great festivals, wells were honoured with a garland of flowers and greenery and dancing took place round them; they became a place for pilgrimage.

With the coming of Christianity, the worship of water spirits was stopped, but because the custom was so deeply entrenched, the decorations, processions and rites continued but they now represented a thanksgiving to god for the gift of water.

Right and below: Graham, who now runs a mind, body and spirit shop in Folkestone's Old High Street made a rather super maypole that fitted exactly into the covenstead, but it turned out to be far more complicated than originally planned. Having made the maypole, the next step was to make it work and this turned out to be even more difficult. Getting the ribbons to weave the right way around the pole took some practise.

When we see well or wall in English place names, it is highly likely that a sacred well or spring had originally been situated there. Amwell, in Hertfordshire, is one example where the ancient springs now help to supply London with water. Ickwell, in Bedfordshire, is another example and this village also celebrates other Pagan customs with festivities, including a Maypole and May Queen on May Day, the old festival of Beltane. Sacred wells also exist in obvious places like Holywell Bay in Cornwall and Holywell, Clwyd, where the well was Christianised as the Well of Saint Winifride. Wells and springs appear in Gaelic and Welsh as tobar and ffynon. Tobermory Bay (Mary's Spring) and Treffynnon in North Wales are examples.

Rock paintings suggest that tree worship was common in the late Palaeolithic period and eventually appeared, in one form or another, in almost every religion and culture. All around the globe people established sacred trees and protected them with considerable ferocity. The Druids and the Norse peoples worshipped in sacred groves and dancing around hallowed trees had an important place in early religious ritual. Dancing round the fairies' tree is often mentioned in old writings. In some places, the tree became an obelisk or pole, as in the Maypole, and was thus a phallic symbol as well. When Christianity succeeded Pagan forms of worship, the importance of the tree became apparent in two ways: the Tree of Knowledge of Good and Evil, of the Old Testament, was given a place of importance and the tree appeared again as the Cross, the sacred tree of the crucifixion. The tree also appears as Yggdrasil, a mighty Ash which was thought to have formed the centre of the world and whose branches stretched out over heaven and earth. We find the tree again as the Tree of Life, a glyph that forms the basis of many magical teachings.

Such was the importance of woods and woodland clearings that many place names refer to them. Probably the most common was the Old English Leah that has become-leigh, -ley, -le or –ly in modern English. The Forest of Arden once covered much of Warwickshire and the villages were built in woodland clearings. Stoneleigh, with its timber-framed houses is one example, as is Elmley, which means elm wood, in Worcestershire. Woodland clearings also appear in place names taken from the Norse language. These have thveit as their root and have often become waite in modern English as in Finsthwaite in Cumbria.

The three gods and the goddess giving their names to the days of the week are also well represented in place names. Tiw or Tiwaz gives his

Standing stones at Avebury in Wiltshire. The signpost by the side of the main road running right through the stone circle is just visible and has been put there because the law demands that it is sited exactly at the right distance from the hazard it is advertising – even if it spoils such an significant early monument. Early man must have had similar rules when it came to placing the stones in exactly the right position and chose big ones so that passing vandals could not easily move them into the wrong position.

name to Tewin in Hertfordshire, Tuesley (Tiw's wood) in Surrey, Tysoe in Warwickshire and Tyesmere (Tiw's Pool or lake) in Worcestershire. Woden gives his name to Wansdyke, the earthworks running through Hampshire and Somerset, Wednesbury in the West Midlands, Wednesfield (Woden's plain) in the West Midlands, Woodnesborough and Wormshill in Kent. Thor/Thunor is found in place names such as Thundersley (Thunor's grove) in Essex. Frigg appears in Lincolnshire as Friesthorpe and as Frogmore in Hampshire, Hertfordshire and Devon.

There appears to be a general agreement among archaeologists that stone circles were associated with the religious beliefs of the late Neolithic and early Bronze Age peoples. The discovery of the bones of animals within a number of sites points to their magical or sacrificial use, but there is also a good deal of evidence, particularly of recent origin, to suggest that there is an astronomical significance to the stones. It seems probable that the practice of religious worship at stone circles was continued long after the emergence of Christianity, and after it was forbidden by the Lateran Council in AD 452. Stone circles are often associated with the Druids who used megalithic sites for their rituals, but the structures are known to have existed at least a thousand years before the time of the Druids. It is thought that the stones could have some connection with ancient fertility religions, for predicting what is likely to happen in a similar way to which we use a calendar these days.

In *Patterns of the Past*, Guy Underwood suggests that single standing stones, like the Neolithic monolith at Rudston in Humberside, were markers for places of exceptional magnetic force and that ancient man regarded such places as sacred. Folklore has always implied that the stones have healing properties and that spirits dwell within them. There are many reports by reliable people of shocks being received when standing stones are touched. Many effects, which tend to substantiate the energy theory of standing stones, were observed during the time of the Dragon Project, a scientific research project set up in 1977 to investigate such phenomena as ultrasonics, radioactivity and force fields around stone circles. During the project, touching an energy node was found to alter the reading on a voltmeter and a Geiger counter registered strong localised areas of high counts. An ultrasonic detector registered pulses of ultrasound at a number of different sites during the pre-dawn periods. These tests were carried out at the Rollright stones in Oxfordshire and the Arbor Low stones in Derbyshire.

Many of the sacred sites in Britain are adjacent to holy hills, some of which have an identifiable relic, which may have been Christianised. Sometimes there is a figure cut into the hillside like the Cerne Abbas Giant, an ithyphallic symbol of fertility cut into the chalk on Trendle Hill in Dorset. There is an earthwork called the Trendle on the giant's hill, and the site of a tenth-century Benedictine Abbey at the foot. Another well-known holy hill is situated at Uffington in Oxfordshire where a huge figure of a horse is cut into the hill. The figure is thought to be connected with the worship of Epona, the Celtic goddess of horses. The horse is above Dragon Hill, which according to legend, is where St George slew the dragon. The Long man of Wilmington is another figure cut into the chalk slopes overlooking the Sussex village and the remains of a Benedictine Priory. On the other hand, of course, the original message of these huge chalk figures could have been nothing more than 'look, we are here – keep out'.

The two major Christian festivals, Christmas and Easter, are Pagan in origin and maintain many of the Pagan customs. In ancient Egypt, on the Winter Solstice, 25 December in the Julian calendar, celebrants would emerge from their shrines at midnight crying aloud, 'The Virgin has brought forth! The light is waxing! The Sun is born!' An infant was held aloft to symbolise

Coldrum Long Barrow near Trottiscliffe in Kent made from huge sarsens. Although sarsen stones were found locally, transporting so many must have involved considerable effort and one wonders what drove early man to such strenuous activities. Were they put there merely to mark some graves or were they used for some other, much more important function?

Note the stark contrasts between the surface soils in the distance, the greens and the white chalk of the path in the foreground. The grey stone circles on the dazzling white must have made a fantastic impression on early man, especially when he viewed such places at night under a full moon.

A white horse carved into the chalk on the side of the Cuckmere Valley near Alfriston in Sussex.

The Long Man of Wilmington near Eastbourne has been carved out of the chalk hills of the South Downs and still stands there as a magnificent sight – even without any form of flashing lights, which are now so popular and almost essential in attracting modern people's attention.

the newborn sun. Fires were kindled to celebrate the birthday of the sun and Christians took part in the festivities. It was therefore expedient to transfer the Christian nativity, which was held on 6 January, to 25 December when the Nativity of the Sun was celebrated.

Mistletoe has been connected with mid-winter festivals since Pagan times. It is one of seven sacred herbs of the Druids and is a symbol of enduring life. The Druids believed that the spirit of the sacred oak lived on in the mistletoe during the winter. As well as being a cure for all illnesses, mistletoe could drive out harmful spirits and bring good luck to anyone who carried it. When mistletoe is hung over a doorway it is a sign of peace and friendship and it was a pre-Christian custom to seal this friendship with a kiss. The age-old custom of kissing under the mistletoe continues today and a kiss can be claimed from any girl standing under the mistletoe, but a berry must be removed and given to her. The early Church forbade the use of mistletoe because of its Pagan origins and many churches today frown upon its use for the same reason.

The use of Druidic Kissing Boughs is a nice custom for the Yule festivities. These are quite large, intricately woven wreaths of mistletoe and fruit that are hung in places where guests pass by. The magical powers of the bough bring good fortune and luck in the coming year. It is to be regretted that large coloured paper garlands have generally taken the place of the kissing bough and houses are often decorated with garish coloured paper chains.

All over Europe the Yule Log was, at one time, perhaps the most important feature of the Christmas festivities. The custom has died out in many places because of smokeless zones and the difficulty of obtaining a suitable log, but it still survives in some country areas. The log, burning brightly on a crisp Christmas night, is a cheerful sight and seems to be particularly appropriate for this festive period, but it is not generally realised that the custom is Pagan in origin. Of course, in the days before central heating, a good burning log provided more than a pleasant sight, it kept the home warm, helped to thaw out workers who came in from the cold and provided welcome light in what was then a dark period of the year.

The log should be of oak, ash or apple. Oak is a sacred wood that was burned in honour of the god Thor. Ash was sacred to Woden and the apple was one of the seven noble trees of the grove. It was to the Isle of Avalon, the secret island of apple trees, that King Arthur went to be healed of his grievous wounds. The log should be kindled at dusk on Christmas Eve with a piece of last year's log saved for the occasion, and it should burn for at

Opposite and right: Trees made a significant contribution to the lives of early man, some helping him and others preventing him from growing his crops. Some trees, especially those with strong growths of mistletoe, were even more mysterious than others.

least twelve hours. The original custom was to keep it burning throughout the twelve days of Christmas, after which it was extinguished and re-kindled at Candlemas, the feast of Imbolg, when it was allowed to burn throughout the day.

The Yule Log is the present day counterpart of the huge communal fires that blazed on the days of the fire festivals and is thus concerned with fertility and driving away harmful influences, as well as being symbolic of the sun. Where open fires are not viable, a candle can be used and should burn all night on a completely fire-proof surface. It should be coloured in accordance with the colour of the day.

Christmas trees, in their role of being the central feature of the celebrations, are a recent introduction imported from Germany in the 1800s, but their origin goes back much further. In Germany, during the late 780s, the English monk, St Boniface, cut down a sacred oak that was worshipped by the Pagans, and in order to placate them, he offered a fir tree to replace the oak. There is also evidence from Egypt, Rome and Greece that trees were decorated during the period corresponding to the Winter Solstice.

The Christmas cake is enshrouded in the mysteries of ancient spells. One such spell was for a girl to bake a cake on Christmas Eve in complete silence. As it was placed in the oven at midnight, the front door of the house was opened and the spirit of the girl's future husband was supposed to enter, walk into the kitchen and turn the cake. The Christmas pudding was originally known as Plum Porage and was a soft product of plums, spices, breadcrumbs and wine. Spirit was poured over the pudding and set on fire as a reminder that, in ancient times, fires were kindled at the Yule festival in honour of the Sun God.

The Star of Bethlehem is symbolised by the star on top of the Christmas tree but its origin is very much older. The five-pointed star, or pentagram, has always been a magical symbol as you have seen in a previous chapter, and of course, the star is a symbol of light and represents the rebirth of the sun.

Wassailing was another Pagan Yuletide custom. This strange word is derived from the Old English wes hal meaning 'to be in good health'. To wassail someone was to drink to their health. The liquor was drunk from a wassail bowl especially on Yule Eve and Twelfth Night. The liquor traditionally consisted of hot-spiced ale with sugar, eggs and thick cream added. When the wassail bowl was large, roasted apples were included and each guest took an apple from the bowl and ate it before wassailing – drinking to the health of all who were present. The wooden decorated bowl was carried round the village by singing wassailers, and in return for an apple or a drink, the villagers would offer a gift. It is regrettable that this old Pagan custom has deteriorated into the present-day bane of 'carollers' voicing a few discordant sounds before knocking at the door for money. (Sadly, since Bill wrote those words, even carol singing seems to have died out in our new multicultural society and traditional Christian carols have been replaced by the latest 'hits' from the pop industry.)

Easter is a Christian festival commemorating the resurrection of Christ and corresponds to the Jewish Passover, but the origin of Easter is very much earlier and stems from the ancient Teutonic goddess Eostre, the Pagan goddess of spring whose celebration was held at the Spring Equinox. Legend tells of Eostre keeping, as a pet, a large beautiful bird that she turned into a hare. The hare, remembering its life as a bird, built a nest on the first day of spring and filled it with brightly coloured eggs – hence the significance of eggs and hares at Easter.

The Old Religion was practised side by side with Christianity for several hundred years during the conversion, and it was prudent, in order to avoid

Above and below: The legend of the Green Man is so ingrained in British folklore that symbols of him crop up in many places, even in some Christian churches.

These pages: Green men and green ladies participating in the Folkestone Charivari. The Green Man, who was supposed to live in the forest with leaves as well as hair, is a widespread symbol for the death, decay and rebirth cycle.

confrontation, to blend existing customs with the new teaching. This is seen in church architecture where the Green Man, a symbol of fertility with protruding tongue, surrounded with foliate branches, is a common feature in many churches and cathedrals. The Green Man also appears on inn signs, sometimes as Jack-in-the-Green, and is often found as a protective symbol by the doors of houses, particularly in country areas

Present-day festivals and fairs are often relics of the past, related to one of the sabbats. The well-known, and well supported, Obby Oss day in Padstow, North Cornwall, begins on May Eve, the feast of Beltane. From the distant past, wells have been venerated because they were the abode of spirits that provided water, which sustained life. To honour the spirits, dancing and festivities took place at the sabbats and the wells were decorated with garlands of greenery and flowers. The custom was so deeply entrenched that it was considered prudent to retain it, but in a Christianised form, and well-dressing ceremonies are found in a number of towns and villages today. Parties and celebrations are plentiful at Hallowe'en, but alas, most of those who participate haven't the slightest idea of the true reason for the celebration – the great sabbat of Samhain.

The teachings of the Old Religion are 'passed from mouth to ear' and those who receive must experience that which is passed. The theme that permeates the whole ethos of the Old Religion is that the mysteries are not learned, they are experienced, and this applies equally to the customs, symbols and icons that can tell us so much about our heritage.

CHAPTER 9

THE TOOLS AND THE ALTAR

Various attempts have been made to explain the origin of the word 'athame' meaning dagger, which is used later in this chapter, but its derivation is unknown. There are a number of references in literature to magical knives. *The Key of Solomon*, translated by Samuel MacGregor Mathers, describes the construction of a black-handled dagger and such items also appear frequently in art. In David Tenier's *The Departure for the Sabbat*, a witch can be clearly seen holding a dagger but the word 'athame' has only cropped up in comparatively recent times.

The tools, or elemental weapons, used in rituals and ceremonies do not possess any intrinsic magical properties. Neither do dowsing rods; they are merely a means of communicating with one's own subconscious. In the Old Religion tools are used to link the witch with the Aristotelian Elements of earth, water, air and fire, which they represent. A good deal of confusion arises due to the controversy concerning two of the tools, the athame or dagger and the wand. The athame should be attributed to the element of fire and the wand to the element of air, but in a number of books this attribution is reversed. Doreen Valiente for example, in her book *Witchcraft for Tomorrow*, uses such a reversed correspondence without giving a reason.

The reversal of the true attribution for the athame and the wand probably originated from the correspondences allotted to the sword and the wand by the Hermetic Order of the Golden Dawn. This magical Order was based primarily on the philosophy of the Qabalah, a secret Jewish mystical tradition, which was developed from hidden meanings in the Old Testament. The Order of the Golden Dawn was founded in 1887 by Dr Wynn Westcott,

Julie making wands. A mug of tea, a sharp knife, sandpaper and some colours are all she needs for making the most attractive wands. Rather than ask the tree whether she may cut some branches, she looks around for already dead twigs and collects them off the ground after the trees have dropped them.

a coroner for north-east London. An aura of hype embraced the Golden Dawn, particularly during the late 1940s and early 1950s when renewed interest in Witchcraft and magic was beginning to emerge and many budding groups utilised their teachings directly or indirectly.

The Golden Dawn attributed the sword to the element of air and the wand to the element of fire and some benevolent writers have suggested that this was a deliberate blind. Francis King and Stephen Skinner, for example, mention this in their excellent book *Techniques of High Magic* and they go on to give the correct ascriptions for the two weapons. The sword of ritual magic and the athame of Witchcraft bear no relationship to each other. In fact, the sword and dagger of ritual magic are also used for different purposes, but in the Golden Dawn, they are both attributed to the element of air.

The athame, like the sword, is customarily made of iron or steel and forged in great heat. Ancient Viking swords were made from thin strands of wire-like iron, twisted together and then beaten for a long time while red-hot so that the bands combine to form one incredible blade. In magic, both the sword and dagger are associated with the red planet Mars, and red is the colour for the element of fire. Michael, the great archangel of fire, carries aloft a huge sword; even if covens wrongly link the athame with the sword, it is difficult to see why they attribute it to the element of air. On the other hand the wand, like the caduceus, is related to the planet Mercury that is traditionally associated with air. Swords are used in many covens and often have symbols from Macgregor-Mathers' translation of *The Key of Solomon* engraved or painted on the hilt, but these are Hebrew symbols, which may be appropriate for ceremonial magic but are certainly not appropriate for the Old Religion. The Farrars, in *The Witches' Way*, believe that the sword is 'ritually exchangeable with the athame' and mention another intriguing use for the weapon. 'When it is necessary, a woman witch may act the role of a man. She symbolises this by buckling on a sword; and she acts as a man, and is regarded and treated as a man, for as long as she wears it'. The sword is not ritually exchangeable with the athame and, in magic, the sword is a weapon associated, on the Tree of Life, with the sephirah Geburah and the planet Mars, but the dagger is attributed to the sephirah Tiphareth and the sun. We of the Old Religion believe very strongly that male and female have distinct, but complementary roles to play; a woman can never play the role of a man or vice versa. We further believe that the sword has no place in Witchcraft; it is basically a weapon used in magic for evocation.

The four basic tools of the Old Religion are the athame of fire, the wand of air, the chalice of water and the pentacle of earth. The pentacle is placed on the north of the altar, the wand on the east, the athame on the south and the chalice on the west.

The athame is a black-handled knife shaped like a dagger about 20-25 cm long. Black, representing spirit, should be shown somewhere on the handle – it doesn't need to be completely black. The blade should be made of iron or steel and, for obvious reasons of safety, the edges and point of the blade should be blunt. Sometimes symbols are engraved or painted on the hilt and this is acceptable as long as the engravings are appropriate. It is very much a personal tool, consecrated and used only by the owner, and should be wrapped in silk when not in use.

The athame is a masculine tool and is used in the symbolic Great Rite of Gardnerian Witchcraft. It is primarily a magical weapon, used in the ritual opening of the circle and the invocation of the Mighty Ones of the four quadrants – north, south, east and west. The 'Mighty Ones' is the phrase used in the Old Religion for the four great Archangels of magic: Auriel in the north, Raphael in the east, Michael in the south and Gabriel in the west. Whether we refer to them as Archangels or Mighty Ones it must be remembered that they are forces, not people.

The magic wand has always been an important part of the paraphernalia of the stage magician. The conjuror waves the wand over a top hat, which has been shown to be empty and, 'hey presto', a white rabbit appears. This is representative of an invocation in true magic in which beings of a higher order are invited into the circle. This is in contrast to evocation in which the magician commands elementals and other beings of a lower order, which have been evoked into the Triangle of Art outside the circle. There is no Triangle of Art associated with the Circle in Traditional Witchcraft. Evocation has no place in the Old Religion. The wand invites, while the dagger or sword commands.

Specific instructions for making a wand can be found in various books. Samuel MacGregor-Mathers' translation of *The Key of Solomon*, for example, says that the wand should be 'cut from the tree with a single blow at sunrise on the day of Mercury', once again indicating that the wand should be attributed to the element of air. It should be made of Hazel and should be from elbow to fingertip in length. Some magical texts say that it must have a piece of iron wire running through its centre for the whole length but never describe just how this can be achieved! Various writers have suggested that a crystal should be incorporated in the wand but the Old Religion has always favoured keeping all accoutrements simple and symbolic so that they can 'speak' to the unconscious mind.

The wand can be made from any reasonably straight piece of wood of a suitable length – elbow to fingertip is a good guide – and, like the athame, it can be marked with appropriate symbols. The wand is a tool used for directing the will and its correct place is on the east of the altar, once again showing its attribution to air. The authority for believing that the wand should be attributed to the element of air arises from the fact that the caduceus was the rod, or wand, carried by the Roman messenger god Mercury or the Greek equivalent Hermes and both are traditionally associated with air. The caduceus is a wand, which is surmounted with two wings and entwined by two serpents very much like the emblem of the medical profession.

The purpose of the chalice is to contain water representing that Aristotelian element. It should consist of a simple metallic cup or a turned wooden vessel; its correct position is on the west side of the altar. It is a feminine tool and, in Gardnerian Witchcraft, is used during the symbolic Great Rite. A chalice is also used in the ceremony of 'passing the mead', which in Traditional Witchcraft takes place just before the closing of every circle. This chalice stands at the centre of the altar from where it is picked up by the High Priest who passes it to the High Priestess for consecration before it is passed round the circle and sipped by all present.

The pentacle is a disc made of metal, wood or stone and should be about 10-15 cm in diameter. It is the tool of the element of earth and should therefore be placed to the north of the altar with a bowl of earth upon it. The altar cloth used in the Old Religion has a pentagram at its centre and the chalice of mead, or anything requiring consecration, stands on this pentagram at the centre of the altar, not on the pentacle.

The cauldron and the besom are the stock-in-trade of the storybook witch and the cauldron also plays a prominent part in Shakespeare's *Macbeth*. In Act IV, Scene 1, three witches, in the middle of a dark cave during a thunder storm, dance round a cauldron chanting:

Double, double toil and trouble
Fire burn and cauldron bubble.

The cauldron and besom are also frequently seen in newspaper or magazine pictures of modern witches, probably because it makes them 'look how witches are expected to look'. The besom was mentioned during the trials of the persecution years when witches were accused of flying to the Sabbat on broomsticks. This was given an air of authority by Heinrich Kramer and Jakob Sprenger, the Dominican authors of *Malleus Maleficarum* (*Hammer of the Witches*) when they mentioned the method of being transported; they 'take unguent which, as we have said, they make, at the devil's instruction, from the limbs of children and anoint with it a chair or a broomstick; whereupon they are immediately carried up into the air'. However, reference to the cauldron during the trials is rare. The reality is probably that both the besom and the cauldron had a simple household function, the broom for cleaning and the cauldron for cooking.

The besom has long been considered to be a masculine implement connected with fertility and suggestions have often been put forward that the act of a witch sitting astride a broomstick was, in fact, a symbolic act representing fertility, in order to encourage the growth of the crops. The cauldron, on the other hand, is considered to be feminine and therefore able to produce. Ceridwen's cauldron, for example, could produce inspiration and knowledge and was able to restore youth.

Cauldrons, used by witches, formed an essential piece of equipment for everyday life and were a valuable part of every household.

The scourge is another item of a coven's equipment that is often prominent in photographs of the altar, but should only be there for use during initiation. The ideal scourge consists of a leather-bound handle with thirteen leather thongs protruding from it. Thirteen in the Fadic numbering system translates into four (1+3) and in numerology the number four signifies the act of creating with thought, a function of the mind and therefore related to Mercury and to the element of air. Some Gardnerian and Alexandrian covens use the scourge rather differently. The Farrars, in their book the *Witches' Way*, say, 'The purpose of the not-too-tight binding and the deliberately light scourging is plain; to help to bring about what may variously be called clairvoyance, expansion of consciousness, opening up the levels, opening up the Third Eye or communion with the Goddess; and, at a more advanced stage, astral projection.' All of these are functions of the unconscious mind and it is difficult to see how scourging can develop them. In the Old Religion, other methods are used to attain access to the unconscious mind and the scourge is used during initiation purely for the symbolic act of cleansing and of 'suffering in order to learn'.

In the Old Religion a necklace made of acorns is always worn by the High Priestess. This is symbolic of fertility and the cyclic processes of nature, which, of course, form the very basis of the Old Religion. It also reminds us that within the acorn is an oak tree with its acorns and so on ad infinitum; a reminder of the continuity of life.

The tools and elemental weapons are used in the rituals and ceremonies of the Old Religion. These take place in an imaginary circle which is cast by the High Priestess following Drawing Down the Moon, the invoking of power into the High Priestess by the High Priest. The High Priest is the magician, the High Priestess the receiver. Some covens, but not Traditional covens, have permanent markings on the floor, often consisting of a double circle bearing the words Tetragrammaton and a couple of words from the Old Testament. In *Witchcraft Today*, Gerald Gardner mentions that the circle is usually 9 feet in diameter with two outer circles 6 inches apart, but as you have seen in an earlier chapter, such a circle is meaningless and has no place in the Old Religion. Gardner does say, however, that the only circle that matters is the one drawn before every ceremony with a duly consecrated magic sword or a knife, but as already mentioned, the sword is not used in the Old Religion.

There is no set size for the circle – it is where the High Priestess casts it. The circle implies that what is within is entirely separate from that without; it is a space in which spiritual work can be carried out completely unmolested by anything outside. The circle of the Old Religion is not to be confused with the circle used in ceremonial magic. In the Old Religion, beings of a higher order are invited into the circle to guard and protect all within, but in magic, entities of a lower order are commanded into the triangle, which is outside the circle. The circle protects the magician while the entities in the triangle are commanded to obey his/her will.

Alexandrian and Gardnerian covens usually place the altar at the northern aspect of the circumference of the circle, as described in the Farrars' *Eight Sabbats for Witches*; in many cases, this means that the altar is outside the circle. It is clear that any dancing, which takes place within the circle, does not encompass the altar. In Traditional Witchcraft, the Old Religion, the altar is considered to be the focal point of all the activity taking place and is consequently located at the centre of the circle where it is able to be circumambulated by dance.

You will see in later chapters that the world 'out there' is simply a projection from ourselves. Everything external – the altar, the tools and the rites – are merely there to 'speak' to the unconscious mind in which the past and the future are one. They are, in fact, the means of realising that the universal forces exist within us: as above, so below. Once we are able to access the unconscious mind, which should be within grasp sometime following third-degree initiation, we no longer require any accoutrements.

In other words the tools are like prompting cards, to help people access the sequence of events or actions. Such tools are also most useful in allowing people to access their own unconscious. When dowsing, for example, the rods or pendulums do nothing more than make this all-important contact. None of the dowsing aids respond to any outside forces. It is the person's subconscious that detects whatever is being looked for. The usual upbringing combined with our frigid education system freezes solid our ability to recognise these subtle feelings inside ourselves. Therefore we need a tool, and the way this tool reacts is determined by our subconscious. Dowsing is also a field occupied by many eccentrics and anyone wanting to explore this most fantastic phenomenon is best advised to make contact with the British Society of Dowsers, whose address can be found on the Internet.

CHAPTER 10

MAGIC AND SPELLS

One eye of a newt,
a wing of a bat,
the tongue of a frog,
the claw of a cat.

This is the brew that the witches in Shakespeare's *Macbeth* concocted before using it to cast a spell that wouldn't do anyone much harm or much good. Spells are used in covens to heal, protect or to bring about a desired situation, but adding brews or potions makes no difference at all. In any case, all the animals mentioned above are local names for plants, but that is hardly relevant for this chapter. It is more important to know that such concoctions are still being used to this day, but without the purveyors of the spell ingredients knowing what magic is. So, what is magic?

There lies within us a vast potential, which can be utilised to change our own lives and make us more able to enhance the lives of others. There are certain techniques that we are able to use by which we can release this hidden potential in order to bring about changes in consciousness and the physical environment. This is magic, exactly the same magic that can be used to harm others or to gain favours for us at the expense of others, but when used like this, it is evil or black magic.

Magic was born with the dawn of mankind and as Bronislaw Malinowski, one of the founders of modern anthropology, says in his book *Magic, Science and Religion*, 'there are no peoples, however primitive, without religion and magic'. But in an evolving world, magic too has evolved and much of what was at one time 'magic' has been absorbed into the realm of orthodox science. Psi-research has become acceptable and Para-psychological laboratories are now established in a number of universities throughout the world. General public interest and awareness in telepathy, clairvoyance and precognition was aroused with the work of Josef B. Rhine, a lecturer in the psychology department at Duke University (Durham, North Carolina, USA), in the mid 1930s. He received a lot of publicity concerning the use of Zener cards (named after Karl Zener, a fellow member of the faculty of psychology at Duke), for research into telepathy and clairvoyance. These cards are now generally known as ESP (extra sensory perception) cards and can be purchased, or better still, made, and used for home research into parapsychology. They are used in covens to encourage and enhance the practice of telepathy.

But what about the magic that is practised in temples and lodges? This has also evolved or, to be more precise, the techniques have evolved; the principles are the same. One thing that certainly hasn't changed, and never will, is the fact that magic is a practical subject. All the reading imaginable will be completely ineffective without practical work: the mysteries are not learned, they are experienced.

Not too long ago it was the vogue in occult lodges to take an oath of absolute secrecy under the most dire threats, and then spend long, boring periods of time practising breathing and relaxation exercises. This was reminiscent of judo clubs that, at one time, spent months teaching nothing but break falls and, in the process, lost many useful members through boredom.

In the same way that judo clubs realised that falling could be taught as an adjunct to the more interesting and spectacular holds and throws, so the more progressive occult lodges reached the conclusion that their neophytes would make better initiates if they were permitted to experience certain aspects of magic from the beginning. This in no way detracts from the absolute necessity of being able to breathe and relax correctly, but it does provide the variety necessary to retain the full interest of the neophyte. The Old Religion employs the use of 'magic' in healing, spells and the creation of amulets and talismans, but witches have never looked upon any of their practices as magic or as anything extraordinary; things that others considered to be magic, or at least strange, have always been natural to the witch. Witches of the Old Religion do not have to practise breathing correctly because they are active. Because they see sex, the great antidote to stress, as a perfectly natural function, they are also happy and relaxed and do not need to practise special relaxation exercises like many magical lodges still do.

It is not the purpose of a coven to get involved in the deeper and more spectacular aspects of magic such as evocation to visible appearance; this is something more appropriate for the esoteric lodge. The magic practised in covens should be confined to that which helps people to live happy, peaceful and productive lives, so that they, in turn, can help and protect others. The magic of the coven is based on the realisation that, from time immemorial, mankind has been aware of a powerful, unseen force which appears to exact some kind of controlling influence over every aspect of life.

Today, we are much more inclined to refer to this mysterious force as luck, but ancient man attempted to control this by means of sympathetic magic; like begets like. An example of sympathetic magic is the fashioning of a love poppet to bring two people together in love. This involves the binding together, with red ribbon, of two miniature dolls which represent the two people concerned. Because the dolls are bound, the couple will also be bound, but the magic should also be enhanced by making the poppet on a Friday, the day of Venus, and perhaps stuffing the dolls with herbs sacred to Venus, such as Heather, Mugwort or Rose. This kind of magic should never be used to bring together two people against the wishes of either. It is an appropriate spell to use for two people who want to be together in love but are experiencing difficulties of one kind or another.

A glance in a dictionary will show that the difference between an amulet and a talisman has never been clearly defined, but the Old Religion does differentiate between the two. An amulet is worn as a charm or mascot to protect against disease, sickness or malefic occult forces, and a talisman is made for a specific purpose. Both should be consecrated and charged magically on the altar, in the circle, or by meditation.

Numerous objects found in Neolithic tombs give credence to the belief that charms were worn or carried by prehistoric man. In ancient Egypt, both the living and the dead wore amulets of various kinds and they played an important role among the Celts. Many examples of Celtic amulets have been found in Britain and the Celtic areas of Europe, the Sun Wheel being a well-known example. The amulet is closely associated with the fetish and fetishism, which appear to be derived from animism in which a soul or spirit is assumed to reside in inanimate matter and in natural phenomena. A fetish is an object, which is believed to have a supernatural potency because it is the abode of a spirit. The word comes from the Portuguese feitico, which is related to magic. Fetishism is the doctrine of a cult, which emphasises the use of fetishes or the belief that spirits may possess objects or persons.

The power residing in an amulet comes through the person who magically charges it by a process that all members of the coven learn to perform. However, many of the first amulets were based on sympathetic magic; the notion that like begets like or that an effect resembles its cause. Because the goat is sure-footed, many tribesman carried a dried goat's tongue or hoof as protection from falling off narrow mountain ledges. Another example of an amulet based on sympathetic magic is that of the scarab, the sacred dung beetle of ancient Egypt. The beetle lays its eggs in animal dung, which is formed into a ball with the egg inside. The ball is then pushed to a place where the heat of the sun will hatch the egg; this was supposed to be symbolic of the life-giving powers of the sun. The scarab, which was dedicated to Ra, the Sun God, was thought to have power over the heart and was thus carried as a personal amulet to ensure long life.

Natural objects such as gemstones or plants can be used either as talismans or amulets. Turquoise, for example, can be used as a talisman with specific power to prevent accidental death, or as a lucky charm or amulet for those born under the sign of Taurus. Since before the Iron Age, jet has been known to exist in abundance around the Yorkshire coast. Jet is fossilized wood or coal, which formed over millions of years; because it is relatively soft and therefore easy to cut or engrave, it has always been popular for making amulets. Being found on the coast, it became a popular amulet among fishermen who carried it as a protection against stormy seas. The Romans thought that jet had an intrinsic magical property, and soldiers carried it for protection and to promote success in battle.

The Vikings of Scandinavia popularised the Runes in Britain, and since each runic letter has a magical significance, they were often used as amulets or talismans. Oak twigs and acorns, often carried as fertility charms, were popular amulets and still are among those who follow the Old Path. The significance of this was mentioned in an earlier chapter when discussing the acorn necklace worn by the High Priestess.

Plants have always been used both as talismans and amulets. During the Middle Ages St John's Wort was often recommended for casting out demons and sprigs of White Heather for luck are often carried in a basket by gypsies and offered to passers by. Amulets of one kind or another can always be found in the homes of those who practise the Old Religion and I cannot imagine that anyone who follows the Old Path would not carry one.

Because talismans are made for a specific purpose, the instructions for making them are also specific and often detailed. The purpose for which a talisman may be made can vary widely. It may, for example, be to get in touch with a particular universal force or one of the elements, or it may be constructed for a more sinister purpose such as compelling the love of another person against their will. More appropriate purposes for the Old Religion are promoting fertility in animals or crops, to obtain knowledge or to recover lost property.

The power, and thus the efficacy, of a properly charged talisman is intrinsic; it is contained within and is very real. Once the talisman has been charged, the power is always replenished from the Universal source by a process of sympathetic magic, hence the necessity for specific and careful construction. Ideally, a talisman, like an amulet, should be constructed by the user, but this is not always possible for a number of reasons, the most likely being that the user is not a person who is able to charge the talisman. A witch may construct and charge a talisman for another person to use, but it is a tradition of the Old Religion that no fee is ever demanded or accepted for this service.

Talismans are often based on the forces associated with the seven 'planets' known to the ancients: Mercury, Venus, Mars, Jupiter, Saturn, Earth and Moon. The twelve signs of the zodiac can also be used but the planets rule these so the latter are considered to be more important. A talisman constructed for matters of love, pleasure or friendship, for example, would contain the sign for Venus as part of its design. Talismans, like coins, consist of a reverse side and an obverse side, which should display the precise intention of the object together with the divine name of the coven. The reverse side should be marked with the symbol of the particular force necessary to bring about, by sympathetic magic, the purpose of the object. A talisman should be kept wrapped in silk, preferably white, and should only be touched by the person for whom it was constructed.

Much of the magic practised in covens is based on the concept of positive thought and its precursor, creative visualisation. Creative visualisation forms the basis of positive thought training, which is used to promote health and to acquire whatever is needed. The technique is not new; there has never been a time when it has not formed the very basis of magical training. Most of the so-called 'popular psychology' books utilise the concept without going into details concerning the principles involved. From the covens and the magical societies, the principle of positive thought has spread to everyday life where excellence is required. Many coaches now realise the importance of training the minds of their athletes in addition to their bodies. A competitor should form a clear and vivid mental picture of winning the event; the more vivid the image is, the greater the chance of action via the unconscious mind. This concept has now also spread into the business world, where it forms a major component in team building training activities.

There is a negative side to the effect of imagination on the mind. It is now known that a large number of illnesses are psychosomatic and this includes some of those that present a more serious threat to health. Negative thought, as well as stress, results in a very real and serious menace to the health of an individual. People can become ill because they believe they have the illness; in the imagination they picture all those signs and symptoms. It has been proven that this can result in physical effects upon the body. Accidents have occurred because the people involved have thought they were going to have an accident. It is a well-known fact that a young child will climb a tree in a garden and generally climb safely down again, but when a parent says, 'you'll fall and hurt yourself' the child often does fall because he/she has formed a picture of falling in the mind. The more vivid the picture formed, the greater the chance of falling.

The efficacy of visualisation is shown by the fact that magical societies springing up in the late nineteenth and early twentieth centuries incorporated the techniques into their rituals. When Theodor Reuss became the chief of the Order of Oriental Templars (OTO), a magical organisation founded by Karl Kellner in 1906, he evolved a teaching consisting of complex visualisation exercises used in conjunction with sexual techniques. Aleister Crowley followed by using the same exercises in his own system of magic, the AA (Astrum Argentium or Silver Star). Crowley was previously a member of the Hermetic Order of the Golden Dawn, which was founded by Dr Wynn Westcott in 1887 and is probably the most famous of the emerging magical societies. The teaching of the Order was based on the Qabalah, which was briefly mentioned in an earlier chapter.

The Qabalah is the theory and philosophy of an ancient system of Jewish mysticism and is the keystone of the Western Magical Tradition. Its origin is unknown but there is some evidence that Daniel (as mentioned in the Bible) brought it from Chaldea, but there is also a legend that it was received by Moses, as a sacred trust, on Mount Sinai. The principles of the secret doctrine of the Qabalah are laid down in the first four books of the Pentateuch. The esoteric teaching is expressed through the Zohar, which was written as a commentary on the Pentateuch and was intended to reveal the hidden meanings of the Biblical narratives. Moses is generally considered to be the author of this work, although there are reasons to suspect that this is a false assumption. However, Moses did initiate the Elders into this secret doctrine, which was then transmitted 'from mouth to ear', which is the literal meaning of the word Qabalah.

Every ancient system of magical or mystical training – the systems taught in the temples and lodges as well as in the Old Religion – has a body of philosophical teachings. Together with these teachings, we also find a symbol having a special significance for the followers of a particular system. Such symbols are the mandalas of some of the Eastern systems, the composite symbol of Raymond Buckland's Seax-Wicca and the pentagram of the Old Religion. (Seax-Wicca is a Saxon branch of Witchcraft, founded in the 1970s by Raymond Buckland after he moved from England to America.) The fundamental basis of the Western Magical Tradition is a rather mysterious looking diagram or glyph known as the Tree of Life. It is a composite symbol often referred to as 'the mighty all-embracing glyph of the Universe and the soul of man'. It is a complete diagram of the Qabalistic system.

The Tree of Life is very much like a filing system; it is said that everything can be placed somewhere on the Tree. There are ten Sephiroth on the Tree of Life, representing divine emanations or different degrees of manifestation, together with twenty-two connecting paths representing the balance or equilibrium of the two Sephiroth they connect. Each Sephirah on the Tree contains the potential of all that come after it. MacGregor-Mathers of the Golden Dawn aptly expressed this when he compared the Sephiroth to acorns; 'hidden in an acorn is an oak with its acorns and hidden in each of these is an oak with its acorns'. In addition to being a body of teaching, the Qabalah, by way of the Tree of Life, its all-embracing glyph, is a practical method of using the mind for a thorough and searching consideration of the nature of the Universe and the soul of mankind.

Whoever wrote the Lord's Prayer was certainly well versed in the Qabalah. On the Tree of Life, the final Sephirah, Malkuth, is the Kingdom, and Geburah and Gedulah form the Power and the Glory. These are the same Sephiroth that form the Qabalistic Cross, which is performed in Alexandrian and some Gardnerian covens during the first-degree initiation, following the 'Drawing Down of the Moon' ritual. There is no doubt that careful and guided use of the Qabalistic method brings the seeker directly into contact with the living powers and forces of the Universe. But it is a foreign and unnecessary intrusion into the Old Religion, and Traditional covens do not include it in any of their rituals. Our sacred glyph is the pentagram.

In the Old Religion, coloured candles, oils, incenses, perfumes and herbs are used in magical operations, but only as correspondences. Like the concoction at the beginning of this chapter, they do not posses any intrinsic power. The power to work magic of any kind is a function of the unconscious mind. From the time of their first initiation, members of Traditional covens are taken through a graduated system of training that enables them to experience the unconscious realms; this leads to magical ability following fourth-degree initiation.

CHAPTER 11
THE UNCONCIOUS MIND

The concept of positive thought training, which was considered in an earlier chapter, postulates different levels of mind. F. W. H. Myers, the Cambridge scholar and one of the founders of the Society for Psychical Research, published a very interesting book in 1903, in which he put forward a theory concerning what he called the subliminal mind. Subliminal comes from the Latin 'limen' meaning a threshold, so the subliminal mind is below the threshold of the conscious mind.

Readers will be familiar with the word 'subliminal' when they recall the great hue and cry, which recurs from time to time, concerning subliminal advertising in cinemas and on television. Myers' theory proposed that the conscious mind was only a part of the complete mind; it was the part of the mind that was above the level of the limen or threshold. In addition to the conscious mind we also posses a level below the limen called the subliminal mind, which is more generally referred to as the subconscious mind or the unconscious as Jung referred to it. The conscious mind is a much later development on the evolutionary scale and is comparatively limited by the necessity for concentration upon the recollections and activities concerned with the struggle for existence.

The unconscious mind is primitive on the evolutionary scale and evolved long before speech. It exercises control over processes that are normally considered to be involuntary and it achieves this via the autonomic nervous system. The autonomic nervous system is usually sub-divided into the sympathetic and the parasympathetic nervous systems. The sympathetic nervous system functions when rapid action is required as in dangerous situations or emergencies; activation of the system causes contraction of the arteries, acceleration of the heart and dilation of the pupils. The parasympathetic system comes into play during rest or sleep and causes dilation of the arteries, inhibition of the heart, constriction of the pupils and it tends to conserve and store bodily resources. Both systems are concerned with such functions as heartbeat, control of the size of blood vessels and glandular secretions, but subliminal consciousness, as will be discussed later, has another important role.

Until the advent of biofeedback in the 1960s, it was considered that the functions of the autonomic nervous system were completely involuntary and the claims of witches, who believed otherwise, were totally unscientific and should be taken with a 'pinch of salt'. Biofeedback involves the use of sensitive electronic instruments, which can detect and feed back information on blood pressure, heart rate, muscle tension, brain wave activity and many other functions. The information is made available in the form of light or sound signals allowing the user to learn to control bodily functions by relating them to the return signal. An example of this is an instrument used to measure the galvanic skin response. This is the skin resistance, which changes in accordance with the body's level of stress. The level of stress is usually indicated by the tone of the return signal and the user consciously attempts to lower the tone and thus lower the stress. The instrument can also be used as a 'lie detector' because lying causes stress and therefore alters the resistance of the skin. The use of biofeedback eventually establishes a mental reaction, which will function independently of an instrument.

Myers is not the only one to have suggested this theory concerning levels of the mind. William James, the American psychologist, said, 'In certain persons, at least, the total possible consciousness may be split into parts which co-exist but mutually ignore each other.' Interest in levels of the mind, other than the conscious, gained momentum with the appearance of psychoanalysis and its derivatives. Freud recognised the Id, Ego and Superego. The Id is that part of the unconscious particularly concerned with inherited, instinctive impulses. It is with us from birth and is responsible for primitive behaviour and self-satisfaction; it continually fights for basic needs and, according to Freud, it is the source of psychic energy.

The Ego ensures that the impulses created by the needs of the Id are compliant with social requirements. It also looks for ways to satisfy the demands of the Id, which will still be socially acceptable. The Superego is that part of the personality concerned with the moral standards demanded

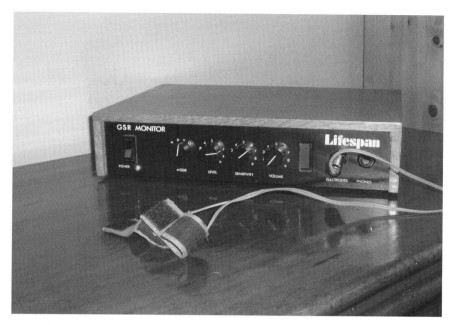

A simple device used for measuring the conductivity of the skin and often used as lie detector. This is useful during some deep relaxation processes because people often cannot determine whether a thought emerging from the subconscious produced a stimulation or whether the stimulation resulted in a thought being formulated. This device will easily determine whether any thoughts from the subconscious were accompanied by emotions.

by society and, initially, by parents; this may conflict with the needs of the Id. Stress can result if the needs of the Id are stifled too much.

C. G. Jung and his theories appear very infrequently in orthodox psychology. This is to be regretted because Jung was very much in rapport with modern physics, particularly the writings of physicists like John Wheeler who has suggested that the mind of the experimenter influences the outcome of an experiment and the experimenter should therefore be called a participator. Wheeler upset some of the scientific establishment when he wrote, 'May the universe in some strange sense be brought into being by the participation of those who participate?'

Like Freud, Jung recognised levels of the mind, but he went considerably further. Jung used the terms psyche and psychic rather than mind and mental because he considered the latter to be primarily associated with consciousness. The term psyche is used for both the conscious and the unconscious, which is compensatory to the conscious. Jung considered the psyche to be as real as the physical, with its own structure and its own laws and involving an energy known as the libido, which constantly flows between two opposite poles. There is a forward movement of this libido, satisfying the demands of the conscious in connection with adaptation to the environment and this is called progression. A backward movement, known as regression, satisfies the demands of the unconscious and is thus concerned with one's inner needs.

Jung travelled widely, meeting 'primitive' tribes in the United States, South America, Africa and India. He studied their religion, folklore and mythology and used these as sources of information concerning the processes of the unconscious. It is not surprising, therefore, to find that the psychology of Jung is in sympathy with the teachings of esoteric philosophy. Processes of the mind were regarded as belonging to two systems. The conscious aspect of the psyche can be likened to the part of an island that is always above water, but there is an infinitely larger part of the island permanently below water that we cannot see and that can represent the collective unconscious. The part of the island that is sometimes covered by the sea can represent what Jung calls the personal unconscious. It can thus be seen that the ego, the conscious, thinking part of the mind, is but a very small part of the total psyche.

The personal unconscious results from repressed impulses from early childhood, repressed desires and forgotten traumatic experiences. It is unique to the individual, depending on personal history and its contents can be aroused into consciousness as in dreams and fantasies. It can also be deliberately aroused by analytic therapy and by certain magical techniques. The unconscious can often emerge uncontrollably into and out of consciousness as a complex with its associated attitudes and emotions that are responsible for certain behaviour patterns. It is essential, for complete health, to bring complexes into consciousness where they can be controlled.

Good hypnotherapists and psychoanalysts, for example, don't like helping people to just stop smoking because they know that they can stop this by mind power alone, but the cause, which created the urge in the first place, is still there and can easily manifest itself by producing some other compulsion. So, rather than treat the symptoms, they prefer their patients to go through a complete analysis to discover for themselves what repressions are responsible for any compulsive behaviour.

The collective unconscious is a vast ocean of tendencies, formed from experiences originating from the remote past of the human race. Jung called these tendencies archetypes and they emerge as imagery and symbols in the dreams of widely different cultural groups, irrespective of the historical period. Dream symbols occur in the folklore and mythology of all cultures and races.

The primordial images of the collective unconscious exercise a potent influence on our lives and this influence is often completely misunderstood because it is unknown to the conscious mind. What is more, the average person will have at least twenty or so of these repressed memories and will be completely unaware that they have that information in their brain. Speech is a comparatively recent evolutionary development and the unconscious levels of the mind predate it by far. Thus, the only way to communicate with the unconscious mind is by the use of symbols; it doesn't understand speech.

The unconscious mind controls vital bodily functions and every thought and action of the human race is impressed in the deeper levels of the collective unconscious, which is, in fact, the astral of the occultists. Therefore, by being able to communicate with our unconscious levels, we are able to avoid psychosomatic illness, possess wealth of knowledge and achieve the things we desire in life. But the unconscious levels of the mind only understand images and symbols and these must be crystal clear and never confused. Thorough training in visualisation is essential to ensure that pictures, images and symbols can be held in the conscious mind with great clarity. The visualising faculty can be used in two ways. We can by the use of creative visualisation, mould the astral to form a matrix which can then be vitalised to create reality on the physical plane, or we can 'tap in' to the astral to gain enlightenment. In the first case it is necessary to visualise, with absolute clarity, whatever is desired and in the second to visualise a symbol and obtain, via the collective unconscious, information concerning that symbol, which has been built up throughout history. Dowsers have the same problem. Imagine one who is looking for water; one would think that this cannot be confused with any other substance, but although the dowser is looking for water, his unconscious mind could be tuned into a tap, a bucket, a hosepipe, a pond, a river or rain and clarity in visualisation is more than essential.

Visualisation plays such an important role in magical operations and every opportunity should be taken to train this faculty. An earnest endeavour should be made to observe things and to be able to recall them in detail. Kim's game is an excellent way to develop this faculty. It afforded an

Kim's Game forms an important part of the training process and can be great help when having to remember things observed during a foraging expedition into the countryside.

important part of the training of Scouts and Guides at one time and consists of covering, say, twenty small objects with a cloth. The cloth is removed and the participants are allowed to view the array for one minute after which the objects are again covered. The exercise entails writing down, in detail, as many of the objects as can be recalled. It is almost incredible to consider that many people look at a watch many times every day and yet cannot recall what kind of numerals it has on its face or even if it has any at all. Try asking your friends what kind of numerals are on their watches. Ask any driver to name the order of lighting in traffic signals, or even whether the red or the green light is at the top. You may be surprised to discover how many there are who do not know. People, generally, are not observant.

Once your visualisation has reached a satisfactory standard, the technique should be put into practice to obtain something that you need. There must be crystal clear visualisation; the object must be intensely and emotionally desired and the will to bring about the desire must be focused on the desired object, which must be earnestly expected. Try it and surprise yourself!

The efficacy of the power of the unconscious mind, or subconscious as it is often called, is made abundantly clear by the fact that people die because they believe they are going to die. In his book *Space, Time and Medicine*, Larry Dossey, M.D. relates the interesting case of a man who was dying for no apparent reason. He had been admitted to hospital as a wizened old man who had dramatically lost weight, but two weeks of intensive examination, including blood tests and X-rays, had shown no abnormalities. During conversation it was discovered that the old man believed that he had been hexed, so the doctors unofficially decided to de-hex him. In a darkened room, a medical tablet was ignited and a lock of the old man's hair was burned in the eerie blue flame from the tablet. During the 'ritual' the patient was told that, as the hair burned and as long as he never told anyone, the hex would be destroyed. The patient immediately showed signs of improvement and completely recovered. This, of course, is the basis of one type of magic; implanting a suggestion into the unconscious mind. The old man had probably been told, following a ceremony such as 'casting the bones', that he was going to die, and this had become fixed in his mind.

In the waking state there appears to be an impenetrable barrier, known as the endo-psychic barrier, between the conscious and the unconscious mind. However, it is not completely impenetrable because we get glimpses of the unconscious during dreams, but if we could break this barrier at will we would be able to gain immediate access to the unconscious and bring it into consciousness. There are methods, known to the magicians and sages of ancient times, by which we can achieve this breakthrough. Those same methods have always been taught in the true esoteric schools, the temples, lodges and covens, but they require intense concentration or intense emotion. The intensity of concentration is difficult to achieve without long training, but emotion can be stirred by the use of ritual, which is why it plays such an important role in magic.

There are three main methods by which the unconscious realms can be experienced: meditation, ritual magic and sexual techniques. The difficulty with meditation is that the process is lengthy and the conscious mind is always too eager to take over; the telephone rings or you wonder whether you are really meditating. Ritual magic requires considerable use of foreign words and phrases – Hebrew in the so-called Western Tradition – and an abundant use of correspondences in the form of incense, perfume, coloured candles, zodiacal gems, correctly coloured robes and, of course, the magical tools. Sex magic involves the body and the conscious mind in bringing about experience of the astral plane via the unconscious mind.

129

It is unfortunate that a puritanical attitude towards sex was the 'order of the day' in western civilisation for a very long time. Mention of anything appertaining to this very natural function is generally taboo, often leading to stressful conscious suppression of sexual desire among couples. This attitude originated from the Church, which insisted that sex was a sin if it was engaged in for any purpose other than the procreation of children. The Church had very good reasons for adopting this stance; large families swelled the ranks ensuring that the coffers never ran dry. The Church dictated that magical aspect of sex was never meant for the masses, however, recent times have seen the emergence of a more liberal point of view concerning sex.

Many articles extolling the virtues of Tantric sex can be found in magazines and newspapers and most give the impression that this is a recent and profound discovery. In fact, sexual techniques have always played an important role in Tantra and in the esoteric inner circles of all persuasions, east and west. The raising of Kundalini, the opening of the Chakras, the manipulation of the chi and the raising of the cone of power, which is conducted in Traditional covens of the Old Religion, can arise from sexual techniques. The similarity between Tantra and the Old Religion is mentioned in Dr Jonn Mumford's splendid book *Sexual Occultism*. I (Bill) met Jonn when we were both browsing in the Atlantis Bookshop during the 1950s. He knew that I was an initiate in the Old Religion, and during the two or three weeks that he was in the UK, he often explained the similarities to the Eastern Tradition. Before leaving the UK for Australia, Jonn gave me a copy of his book, a passage from which I quote below:

> Startling similarities between Tantra and modern witchcraft indicate that the primal layers of the unconscious in east and west seek satisfaction in an earth cult which is matriarchal and feminist. These common features are couched in the symbolic language of myth and allegory, which is a form of communication beyond time, history, science and logic.

As Jonn points out in his book, orgasm is an extremely important psychophysical function that frees the physical body from tension and removes psychic blockages, allowing the blood and the subtle energy associated with the chi to circulate freely. The ecstasy of orgasm can create detachment from the ego and provide a glimpse of the Absolute, samadhi of the Eastern Tradition. This brief moment of timelessness is the key to sexual magic; whatever is held vividly in the imagination at the moment of orgasm will materialise on the physical plane.

I don't want to create the impression that sex magic is an easy option; it certainly isn't. It necessitates a close rapport between the participants, both of whom must have achieved a good degree of sexual awareness, and it requires the psyche of both to be completely free of negative attitudes towards sex; they must be free from the shackles of convention, inhibition and guilt. Initiates of the Old Religion may begin to learn the appropriate techniques and procedures following third-degree initiation and may be ready to use them in magical operations following fourth-degree initiation. Certain techniques, those that are necessary for a successful third-degree initiation are sometimes taught and practised following second-degree initiation. It would not be right for me to enter into a detailed discussion on the techniques of sex magic, some of which are closely guarded. The correct place for this is the coven.

CHAPTER 12

THE ETHERIC AND ASTRAL PLANES

The Old Religion employs magic for healing and spells and the fundamental precept of magic is that the physical universe is the densest of a number of 'planes' or levels, all emanating from one source, the Creator. These planes, which consist of interlocking and interdependent vibrational systems, exist within precisely the same confines as the material universe, but are discrete from it and we are not normally aware of them during waking consciousness. They are usually designated as the physical, etheric, astral, mental and spiritual planes. From the point of view of the Old Religion, the two most important planes are the etheric and the astral.

The etheric plane is essentially an energy network linking the physical body to the astral body. The etheric body, or etheric double, so called because it is a duplicate of the physical body, resides on this level and is intimately concerned with health, and the absorption and distribution of the 'essential life force'; it is the level where we find the acupuncture points and the chakras, the subtle psychic centres that create a bridge between mind and the material, the universal and the individual. The existence of the etheric body has long been accepted in esoteric teaching and is in accord with the Chinese concept of an energy system existing in and around the body. Pictures from early Egypt, Rome, Greece and India show holy figures in a luminous surround long before artists painted saints with halos. This energy field is thought to dissociate itself from the physical body during sleep, meditation and hypnosis, and when the body dies.

Research in the USA and the old Soviet Union has suggested that a force field surrounds the body and the 'phantom leaf' experiment of Kirlian photography not only seems to prove the existence of this field but also shows that it remains for a while following the removal of a piece of the leaf. Kirlian photography originated in 1939 following an observation made by Semyon Kirlian, a Russian electrician, when he visited a research institute to collect an instrument for repair. While at the institute he saw a demonstration of electrotherapy using high-frequency apparatus and noticed how flashes of light jumped between the electrode and the patient's skin. Kirlian decided to construct a generator which would produce a frequency of up to 200 KHz (200,000 cycles per second), and to place a photographic plate between the electrode and his hand. The plate showed myriad of flashing lights arising from the bioluminescent image of his hand. Kirlian, together with his wife Valentina, continued to experiment and it appeared that all living things generated a bioluminescent field that became visible when they were placed in a high-frequency electric field.

The Russians were the first to report the strange phantom leaf effect in which a portion of a leaf was removed prior to a Kirlian photograph being taken. The Kirlian photograph showed an image corresponding to the leaf as it was before the piece was removed, suggesting that an energy matrix for the complete leaf exists for a period after the piece of leaf has been removed. This phenomenon has been put forward as an explanation for the so-called phantom limb experience of amputees, in which people who have lost an arm or a leg sometimes complain that they can feel pain in the missing limb and have a sensation that it still exists.

More than five years before Semyon Kirlian developed a method for recording the field, Harold Saxton Burr, a neuro-anatomist, carrying out research at Yale University, postulated that an electrodynamic field was responsible for forming the matrix or mould for manifested life. Together with F. S. C. Northrop, he published a paper on Life Fields (L-Fields) in the 'Quarterly Review of Biology' in 1935. Burr devoted over thirty years to the investigation of etheric fields and published an interesting book *Blueprint for Immortality* in 1972. He thought the fluctuation in voltage in these fields gave advanced warning of disease, which could then be treated before manifestation occurred. This research has vindicated the writings of Baron von Reichenbach in 1845 and Dr Walter Kilner in 1912 and given some credence to the claims of sensitives, that they could perceive an aura surrounding human bodies. Baron von Reichenbach was the discoverer of creosote, but from our point of view, his more important discovery was a strange energy, which he called Od, emanating from humans.

Dr Kilner carried out scientific research on the aura while he was working at St Thomas's hospital in London, but medical authorities generally discredited his work. When the aura is observed, it can be seen to consist of three fairly distinct parts: the etheric double, the inner aura and the outer aura. The etheric double is a dark band completely enveloping the body and extending outward to between one and two centimetres. It is a prominent feature and was first regarded as an optical illusion, but it was noticed that it alters with the same person under different conditions. Sometimes it is very conspicuous, but at other times, screens may be required to see it. The inner aura is an emanation, which like the etheric double, follows the contours of the body and extends outwards to about ten centimetres. It appears, particularly when screens are used to view it, to give a shimmering effect, rather like a mirage. The outer aura consists of a hazy cloud extending beyond the inner aura for some fifty centimetres or more, giving an overall egg shape to the total observable aura. The aura appears wider at the head than at the feet and appears to project from the fingers. According to Dr. Kilner, 95 per cent of people, using correct techniques, can see the aura. Although it is possible to see the aura by direct vision of a subject against a dark background, the sighting is facilitated considerably by the use of aura goggles or Kilner screens, in which the lenses are stained blue with dicyanin. Some people cannot see auras against a dark background but can see them clearly, without screens, against a white background.

Looking at auras is an activity that is often carried out during coven meetings, but it can also be practised quite safely at home. The hands, with the fingers spread and the tips of one hand almost touching those of the other hand, should be held against a dark background. If the fingers are moved slightly apart, it is often possible to see streams of blue-grey luminescence running from the fingers of one hand to the fingers of the other hand. A narrow glow may also be seen surrounding each hand. It may be easier to see the glow of the aura if the eyes are first sensitised by looking at a white wall through coloured, transparent plastic. Try both blue and red. It also helps if the eyes are focused slightly behind the subject being observed. (Note that is similar to the way those patterns with 3-D imagines embedded in them become visible.)

The astral plane lies immediately beyond the physical plane but is 'connected' by the nebulous etheric body discussed above. Its basic 'material' is known as the astral light or akasha and it pervades the whole of space and interpenetrates everything within. This tenuous 'substance' cannot be perceived by the normal senses because its particles vibrate at such a high rate and it lies in a totally different plane of existence. The astral light can be manipulated in order to control the dense matter of the physical plane or to form a matrix for materialisation on this plane.

Every thought, word, deed and action is indelibly implanted in the astral light and can be retrieved via the unconscious mind which allows access to the astral realms and everything implanted in the astral light. As already mentioned, some eastern traditions refer to this all-pervading spiritual 'substance' as akasha, hence the term akashic records. It was briefly mentioned in an earlier chapter that if a number of people with the same ideals and modes of thought function together as a group, for example in a coven, a pattern will emerge forming a group consciousness, which will be implanted, in its entirety, in the astral light. This pattern is known as an egregore, which is a group thought-form, a living entity in the astral light. When a particular ritual is used by a group and has been for many years, the egregore that has been built up over this time span can become extremely powerful because it is composed of all the thoughts, ideals, emotions and concepts of those who have been affected by that ritual. For this reason, the opening ritual in traditional covens never varies and, when the ritual has been performed, there is immediate contact with the egregore, inculcating depth and influence for the whole meeting.

Other thought-forms can be built up by the imagination in which the power of the mind forms a mental image that will be impressed in the astral light; if the appropriate emotion associated with this image is created, it forms the basis for magic. In the Old Religion, specific training of the pictorial imagination forms an important part of coven work following third-degree initiation. The power of thought cannot be too strongly expressed. If, for example, a person thinks strongly enough of being in a certain place at a certain time, he/she will appear in that place.

The astral counterpart of the body resides on the astral level and can be dissociated from the physical body to travel on the astral plane. Everything has its astral counterpart but laws appertaining on the physical plane do not apply on the astral plane; time and space are absent. But, what is time? We speak often with great enthusiasm about the way we enjoyed our last holiday, which is now in the past, and we look forward with relish to our next holiday, which is in the future. We talk of the past and the future because we are living in the present. But are we? The present is the dividing line between the past and the future but the present is illusive for, if we believe that everything exists in time, the present doesn't exist at all!

We can speak of the past, right back to the Big Bang (the instant at which time and space came into being) if we so desire, and we can easily comment on anything which occurred, say, three weeks, three months or three years ago. We can also envisage the future as far into the distance as we feel inclined, just as we envisage the next full moon or the next leap year.

Whether we imagine the past or envisage the future, we are thinking in terms of measurable periods of time, but the present has no such dimension. However small we care to think of the present, even if it is infinitesimally small, it can always be divided into a past and a future. The only way in which this cannot apply is if the present is a dimensionless instant; then, of course, it doesn't exist. Before we examine the significance of this and its relevance to the work of a coven, the occult and certain paranormal phenomena, a brief excursion into the subject of time from a scientific aspect may be beneficial.

The concept of time, in western thought, is that we move inexorably forward from birth to ultimate death. Along this arrow of time we live in what we believe to be the present, leaving the past behind and looking forward to the future. This view was given credence by the mechanical model of the universe proposed by Sir Isaac Newton in 1687, which formed the basis of physics for the best part of 300 years.

Newtonian physics, classical physics as it is known today, appealed to common sense and is still valid today. Space was absolute and fixed and time was also absolute; a separate entity, which flowed from the past to the future, the present moving along with the flow. In classical physics an event was an event, and as long as clocks were accurate, a particular event occurred at precisely the same time for all observers. A clock that was moving kept the same time as an identical clock that was stationary.

With the dawn of Einstein's Special Theory of Relativity in 1905, an entirely new concept of time appeared; time and space were totally inseparable as a space-time continuum and there was no unique, universal or absolute time. Time was personal and depended upon where a person was and how that person was moving.

If someone is moving past you your watch tells you what is known as the proper time, but an identical watch carried by the person passing appears, to you, to run more slowly; this is relative time. The greater the speed, the more pronounced this discrepancy becomes. This is not simply an illusion. It is a reality, which has been measured and is exemplified by the so-called twins paradox in which one twin stays on Earth while the other twin makes a journey in a spacecraft. When the astronaut twin returns to Earth, the Earthbound twin is very much older; about seven times older if the spacecraft had been travelling close to the speed of light. The Special Theory of Relativity has shown us that time is relative and thus sooner, later, now and simultaneous are all relative terms. Time and space are inseparable as St Augustine suggested when he said, 'Time is a property of the universe that God created.'

According to modern physics we appear to interact with aspects of the material world as we move through space-time and this can be plotted on a graph where it is known as our world line. Yet the reality is that the events that make up space-time already exist. Only a time flowing in a one-way fashion involves a past and a future.

Time does not flow; the arrow of time (time flowing only one way and its consequence, the present) is a property of our conscious mind – an illusion.

Occult science has always asserted that the world we see 'out there' is an illusion and this is also found in the eastern concept of maya, a Sanskrit term meaning illusion. On the evolutionary scale, the conscious mind is a more recent development than the unconscious mind and is susceptible to suggestion, making it prone to conditioning by teaching or the media for example. The unconscious mind, on the other hand, always tells the truth but is seldom listened to. The unconscious mind is also linked to the astral plane, or the collective unconscious as Jung called it, and this is why it plays such an important role in magical operations. It wouldn't be amiss for a physicist to ask whether the astral plane had any connection with the space-time continuum in which events don't happen, they just are. The question may not, however, receive a standing ovation among establishment scientists.

The unconscious mind comes into play during sleep when, in our dreams, we glimpse what may be a vista of space-time. Perhaps those who see a ghost have momentarily, and without realising it, broken down the barrier of the present. UFOs may already exist in the fabric of space-time and are seen by those whose consciousness has been temporarily raised to a point where this very arbitrary and dimensionless barrier, which we call the present, ceases to exist, and time and space are one. In his excellent book, *The Tao of Physics,* Fritjof Capra quotes an apt and beautiful passage from Swami Vivikananda's *Jnana-Yoga.* 'Time, space and causation are like the glass through which the Absolute is seen. In the Absolute there is neither time, space nor causation.'

It is difficult to subdue the conscious mind during normal waking consciousness due to the myriad stimuli to which we are subjected. However, there are methods, taught in the covens, which enable the so-called endopsychic barrier to be crossed, giving access to the unconscious mind and hence to the astral plane.

Our consciousness can be transferred to the astral body and information can thus be obtained from any area that is visited by the astral body. This is the basis of so-called remote viewing that recently made headline news when a former US soldier claimed that it was being used for intelligence gathering. The dissociation of the astral body from the physical body can be brought about intentionally, as in astral projection, or it can occur spontaneously when it is known as an out-of-body-experience or OOBE. With suitable training, the transition between the physical and the astral can be established by will when required, and this forms an important aspect of coven work.

As mentioned above, it is possible to 'tap into' the astral but only via the unconscious mind, which does not understand language; it can only function by the use of symbols or images. Thus by meditating on a symbol, such as a pentagram, we are able to contact the astral, via the unconscious mind, and obtain feedback on everything that the pentagram has ever meant to the human race from the birth of its significance, including any emotions associated with it. Symbols are either simple geometrical forms or more complex patterns built up from simple geometry like the alchemical concept of the squared circle or the linked triangles found in many mandalas. They can, and ideally should, be thought of in three dimensions. Many of Jung's writings emphasise the importance of symbols: 'a sign is a substitute for, or representation of the real thing, while a symbol carries a wider meaning and expresses a psychic fact which cannot be formulated more exactly.'

An example of practical magic, which utilises the astral light, is the method used, but not explained, in most of the popular 'psychology' books of the *How to Use the Mighty Power of the Mind* variety. They are based on the assumption that anything needed can be acquired if it is imagined to be already possessed, but it is difficult to imagine any object if it cannot be clearly visualised. You have seen how visualisation plays an extremely important role in magical operations, and covens give a high priority to fostering, among their members, an earnest endeavour to observe things and recall them. As mentioned in the previous chapter, Kim's game is a very effective way to train the visualising faculty and plays an important role in the work of the coven.

As previously mentioned, the astral light, the basic 'material' of the astral plane, can be manipulated to form the matrix for materialisation on the physical plane. This is achieved by visualisation, which can be aided by photographs or drawings of the object or condition desired. The matrix then has to be filled with energy by means of the two poles, feminine desire force and masculine will power. To summarise this operation:

1. There must be absolutely clear visualisation of whatever is desired. All the senses must be used: you must see, feel, hear, smell and taste the desired object if these senses apply.
2. The object required must be intensely desired – to the point of emotion.
3. The will must cause the action to bring about the desire and must be focused in a narrow beam. In other words, there must be unwavering concentration on the desired object.
4. The object desired must be earnestly believed to already exist.

This is the very basis of magic; all the teaching disseminated by Traditional covens is directed towards breaking down the endo-psychic barrier to attain access to the astral via the unconscious mind.

CHAPTER 13

DIVINATION

If you look in a dictionary for the definition of divination, you will probably find something like 'the art or practice of divining, seeking to know the future or detecting hidden things by supernatural means.' But what do we mean by the future? As you saw, in the previous chapter, the future is separated from the past by a very arbitrary dimensionless barrier which we call the present, the now. The past and the future can be any determinate length of serial time, but even if we allotted it the minutest period of time, the present could still be divided into a past and a future so it must be dimensionless.

The Tantric mystics of Tibet believe that our perceptions of the Universe existing in time are incorrect and Buddhists also recognise a world that exists beyond time, but because we apparently experience past, present and future linearly and sequentially, it is no surprise that we interpret time as absolute. We appear to live in an eternal present as we progress along the arrow of time. We are trapped between the future and the past in an immeasurable present because, however small we make that present, we would be living in the past and the future simultaneously.

There is no present, except in the conscious mind, and consequently, there is no future and no past. Every event and time is fixed in the unity of space and time, which is, as you have seen, known as space-time. Space is concerned with locations; space-time is concerned with events. Long before the appearance of the Relativity Theory and quantum physics, the magicians of old were able to 'see' this panorama of events in the astral by entering the unconscious mind where the present is no longer a barrier between the future and the past.

If these times and events already exist in the fabric of space-time or the astral plane, does this mean that our lives are predetermined? No, because we have seen, in a previous chapter, that it is the matrix of materialisation that exists in the astral light, which is the 'material' of the astral plane, and this has to be moulded by the will before being filled with mentative energy which results in its materialisation on the physical plane.

John Wheeler, the great Princeton University astrophysicist who has made significant advances on Einstein's Special Theory of Relativity, has suggested that the observer literally creates the Universe by his/her observations. He made this clear when he said, 'may the Universe, in some strange way, be the creation of the created?' Progressive statements of this nature obviously don't elicit a round of applause from many scientists of the old school. However, Wheeler upset the scientific establishment even more by suggesting that the quantum principle shows that, in a sense, the observer's future actions define what happens in the past, even if that past is so remote that life did not then exist. With no knowledge of Relativity Theory or Quantum Mechanics, witches from the distant past have always believed that we make our tomorrows; this is just about what Wheeler has told us and what many modern scientists believe.

Divination shows us a tendency for a certain event to occur because the matrix is already there, and this gives us the option to use our will to avoid this event if we so desire. In this respect, we make our tomorrows, and if we take note of any obstacles conveyed to us by divination, our passage through life should be a smooth one.

From almost the beginning of time, it has been the desire of mankind to predict the future. Although many people today would deny that they have any belief, or even interest, in divination, those same people often consult their stars daily in the newspapers, enter the palmistry or fortune-telling booths 'just for a laugh' when at the seaside or secretly consult a tarot reader or rune master.

There are many different methods of divination practised today but these can broadly be divided into two main groups:

1. Deductive divination.
2. Intuitive divination.

Astrology, physiognomy (the art of judging character by appearance, particularly of the face), chiromancy (divination by reading the hand),

Runes hold such magic powers that they are still banned in Germany, although they represent nothing more than an ancient alphabet. The National Socialists in Germany attributed great value to them and they can be used all manner of purposes including divination. Learning something about their significance is not terribly difficult and many people find them helpful for all manner of purposes.

palmistry (divination by the lines on the palm) and graphology (reading character by hand-writing) are examples of deductive divination. Clairvoyance (the faculty of seeing mentally what is happening out of sight), clairaudience (the faculty of hearing mentally what is inaudible), cartomancy (divination by playing cards, which includes the tarot) and reading the Runes are all examples of intuitive divination. The I Ching, divining wheel, crystal ball, tea-leaves, dowsing rods and the pendulum are also concerned with divination.

It must be emphasised again that every method of divination used to foretell future events concerning a person can only show whether that person is predisposed to an event occurring. The position of the heavenly bodies, for example, predisposes a person to a certain course of events but they do not compel the person to adopt that course because everyone possesses free will. This does not nullify the use or effectiveness of astrology that can warn us in advance that there is a tendency for a certain course of events to occur. With this foreknowledge we can act appropriately.

Whatever method of intuitive divination is used, information concerning the tendency of a future event is retrieved from the astral plane, via the unconscious mind, into the conscious mind of the reader from which it can be passed on to the enquirer. However, the conscious mind does not have direct contact with the astral plane; it has to work via the unconscious mind where the barrier of the present does not cause a problem. As you have seen in a previous chapter, there are various methods for achieving access to the unconscious mind and these are taught in covens, but some systems of divination have their own inbuilt facilities, which assist this. A notable example can be found in Tarot decks in which the cards can 'speak' to the unconscious mind. This is why it is better to use a simple, highly symbolic deck like the Marseilles, IJJ or Rider Waite rather than a beautifully artistic deck such as the Salvador Dali.

Unlike the majority of Tarot decks, there is no evidence that any individual created the Marseilles deck so, in this respect alone, it doesn't embody the character or persuasion of any one person. Because of its great simplicity, the Marseilles deck presents an ideal opportunity to enter the realms of the unconscious mind by meditating on the cards. The best card to begin with is card II, the High Priestess, which is the card of wisdom. It is most enlightening to meditate, in time, on all of the twenty-two cards of the major Arcana.

When carrying out a divination with the tarot, there are numerous operations that must be performed prior to the actual reading. The reader should observe the client surreptitiously to ascertain his/her state of mind and look for any signs of nervousness, anxiety or tension. This is best done while talking to the client because the voice is a good guide to the state of mind. In conversation it is also possible to obtain information, which will help with the evaluation of the forces and trends shown in the cards. The cards must never be interpreted to fit any information gleaned from the client.

All divination should employ the intuitive and imaginative faculties to a very large extent. In fact, the opening of the mind to an intuitive perception is aided by the act of divination. It is absolutely essential that a diviner should enter upon divination with a completely clear and unprejudiced mind. Cards should be handled as often as possible in order to get the 'feel' of them, and as mentioned above, it is also useful to meditate on them.

It is most important to realise that anyone touching the cards influences them in some way, just as an experimenter influences the outcome of an experiment and is better described as a participator. This is why, during a Tarot reading, it is essential that the client shuffles and cuts the cards. In occult terms, the client's thoughts and feelings will be impinged on the astral light and the reader will receive this information via the partnership of the unconscious mind and the symbolism of the appropriate cards. This makes clear the importance of consecrating the cards before any Tarot reading is entered upon.

The Runes are another example of the important role that symbolism plays in gaining access to the unconscious mind for the purpose of divination. They are, in fact, keys that unlock the unconscious mind releasing the wisdom and magic that reside there. Edred Thorsson makes this point very clear in his excellent book *At the Well of Wyrd*, 'anyone who takes the time to become skilled in rune casting will open unseen channels between the conscious and unconscious selves.'

Great variation is found in the number of runes forming the alphabet in different countries. This is because new shapes were used to accommodate the different sounds encountered as they moved from their North Italic origin into Germany and Scandinavia, and then to Britain. New sounds were developing, particularly during the seventh and eighth centuries and, instead of creating new symbols for these sounds, the same rune was often used for several related sounds causing some runes to fall into disuse. This happened in Scandinavia where two of the runic alphabets, the Danish and Swedish, consisted of only sixteen runes. In contrast, the Anglo-Saxon settlers in Britain increased the alphabet to thirty-three runes. The Common Germanic runes are generally used in Traditional covens for the purpose of divination; the first six runes of this twenty-four-rune alphabet give rise to the more usual name of F U T H A R K.

The esoteric aspect of the runes is found in the mythology associated with the god Odin, the Germanic god Wotan. Odin is said to have gained his secret knowledge of the runes by hanging, without food or water, for nine days and nine nights on the World Tree, the great sacred Ash, Yggdrasil. The most significant aspect of this belief is that Odin was pierced with his own spear, a voluntary sacrifice in order to obtain the secret hidden knowledge. This is described in 'Havamal', the second poem in the *Elder Edda*. The *Elder Edda* is the older of two Scandinavian books and consists of a collection of ancient mythological and heroic songs and poems.

I know I hung
on the windswept tree,
through nine days and nights.
I was stuck with a spear
and given to Odin,
Myself given to myself.
I peered downward,
I took up the runes.
Screaming, I took them.
Then I fell back.

Odin's act of self-sacrifice, in order to obtain the secret knowledge, is consistent with the esoteric teaching of the Old Religion in which initiation ceremonies through the five degrees are undergone by the neophyte. All these initiation ceremonies, in one way or another, symbolise the death and rebirth of the initiate and they are the culmination of a series of trials, ordeals and terrors, which must be faced in order to gain possession of the secret knowledge. This period of self-sacrifice involves the physical, mental and spiritual faculties.

There are a number of popular books on the market that tend to confuse readers. They mix the names of the runes, giving some Common Germanic names with a few Old English and Old Norse names thrown in. Some books also give a mixture of symbols and there are sets of runes available that are combinations of various alphabets. For divination purposes it is essential to use a set of runes that is not mixed, preferably Common Germanic. It is a good idea to make your own natural runes like those shown. As with the Tarot cards, the best way to achieve success with runic divination is to handle them as often as possible so as to get the 'feel' of them. Nine runes should be held in the cupped hand prior to casting on a cloth. All the positions and any inverted runes should be carefully meditated on and absorbed into the unconscious mind, which will then receive any information from the astral plane and refer it to the conscious mind when it can be passed on to the enquirer.

I can hear the reader saying, 'He has told us about the Tarot and the runes but hasn't told us what the various cards and rune staves mean in a reading.' Successful divination cannot be achieved by learning a specific meaning for any card or rune: this will be conditioned by the whole of the spread. All divination must involve the unconscious mind, which is in touch with the astral plane where the whole panorama of time and events is set out.

The spread of the Tarot cards or the casting of the runes will 'speak' to the unconscious mind, which will then provide the answer to a possible problem or any predisposition to an event.

Traditional covens of the Old Religion attach great importance to the practice of divination and witches in these covens are required to show considerable ability in this calling before they can be considered for initiation into the third-degree element of air. The method used for divination is left to individual choice. It may be one of the lesser-known methods such as reading the teacup or divining by a handful of pebbles thrown onto a flat surface. Scrying by peering into a crystal ball or magic mirror, like the typical storybook witch, is probably the most widely known form of divination and is still popular in Traditional covens that I have come across. A magic mirror can be formed from a convex or concave mirror resting on a black cloth, a pool of ink or simply a bowl of water, in which case it is better that the bottom of the bowl is coloured black. Whatever method is used, it must never be practised by rote learning. The very essence of any form of divination is by way of the unconscious mind and this is, in fact, the basis of all teaching in the Old religion. Being a witch entails doing, not simply attempting to learn by reading. In a Traditional coven you are taught in accordance with the occult maxim, 'the mysteries are not learned, they are experienced'.

As in the dictionary definition, divination also includes the process of seeking and finding hidden things. The tools usually used by the witch to achieve this are the pendulum or dowsing rods. A pendulum can be made by attaching practically any form of weight to a piece of string – a stone with a hole in it is ideal. A more sophisticated beech-wood pendulum is provided with a cavity in which can be placed a sample of the substance that it is desired to detect, but a simple weight on the end of a string is just as suitable. If the end of the string is held between the forefinger and thumb the pendulum gyrates in a way that is characteristic for any substance over which it is suspended and, once this is known, anything associated with that substance can be detected. The same is true for dowsing rods, which can also give a specific reaction for any situation, thus allowing missing or hidden things to be traced. The traditional divining rod was a forked twig of hazel. One branch of the fork is held in each hand and the twig bends upwards when water is located. Rods now tend to be L-shaped and the short part of the L is held allowing the rod to turn when a hidden object is located.

Governments and large companies pay huge fees to dowsers who are able to pinpoint the location of water and metals, so we can assume that dowsing does work but no satisfactory explanation of how it works has ever been put forward. There seem to be three major theories regarding this:

1. Everything emits some kind of radiation that causes a change of tone in the muscles of the forearm and it is this effect that causes the apparatus to respond.
2. The dowser emits radiation, which can be reflected back, like radar, causing movement of the pendulum or rod.
3. The movement of the pendulum or rod is due to an unknown force that is received by the unconscious mind, which then directs the movement of the apparatus.

The efficacy of dowsing with rods was convincingly demonstrated to me by Hamish Miller in 1990 when I had taken a team to Somerset to investigate a strange force which had invaded the lives of Frank Pattemore and his son Nigel at their home, Iverson Cottage, in Somerton. Hamish and Paul Broadhurst had just written *The Sun and the Serpent*, an investigation into Earth Energies by tracking the St Michael Line, a ley line formed by the alignment of St Michael's Mount, Glastonbury and many other legendary places including Avebury and Bury St Edmunds.

Because the St Michael Line ran through Glastonbury, only a short distance from Somerton, I had contacted Hamish in case he was interested in the investigation of the bizarre occurrences at Iverson Cottage. Extensive investigation had been conducted by the South-Western Electricity Board, the Electrical Research centre at Capenhurst, ghost hunters, spiritualists and strangers in dark suits, all to no avail. My team consisted of two physicists, an electrical engineer and a radio engineer. We took with us some reasonably sophisticated and expensive equipment, with which we discovered and measured a force that intermittently appeared to run diagonally across the lounge in Iverson Cottage and gave rise, during its presence, to high voltage surges on the domestic supply, sometimes reaching 3kV. This force burnt out bulbs, TVs, cookers, heaters and, surprisingly, destroyed battery-powered equipment. We anxiously awaited the arrival of Hamish and Paul.

Hamish is a blacksmith and metal sculptor, and a highly experienced dowser. Following tea and biscuits, during which time nothing was mentioned concerning the strange force we had measured, Hamish asked whether he could dowse Iverson Cottage. Frank Pattemore readily agreed and, within moments, Hamish said, 'there is a very strong Earth Energy running diagonally through this room.' With dowsing rods made in his forge, for probably no more than a couple of pounds, Hamish had discovered the same intermittent force that we had found with our expensive scientific equipment. Yes, there is no doubt that dowsing does work.

This chapter is not intended to give the reader details concerning the practice of any form of divination: such information should be sought from a specialised source, which can certainly be found in Traditional covens. The purpose of this book is merely to describe the activities, which will be encountered in a coven of the Old Religion where you learn by being shown and then experiencing rather than by reading from a book.

It might also be worth bearing in mind that when asking anyone to give a reading by any of the methods mentioned above, it would be advisable to ask first for the reader's summary of what had gone on in your life during the past few months; there is no point in asking for any further details if this is not satisfactory. What is so astonishing is that there are a good number of people who are capable of providing astonishingly accurate information, despite not knowing the person for whom they are giving a reading. As far as dowsing is concerned, the British Society of Dowsers can be found through the Internet and their meetings and courses are excellent. Once starting out on your own, it is essential to use the divination for determining information, which can be verified almost immediately. That way one can see how accurate the divination is. It is also important to remember that dowsing rods, runes, Tarot cards and the like are all open to interpretation and it is exceedingly easy to get an accurate result with a faulty understanding. Therefore carefully controlled experiments are vital in helping a beginner develop his faculties. Another problem with things like dowsing rods and pendulums is that they can easily be controlled by your own subconscious. Therefore there is no point in dowsing anything in which you are emotionally involved. You are very likely to get the result you are looking for; to get at the truth it is best to have someone else dowse on your behalf.

The strange point is that no one has yet explained how divination works. Many scientists won't even attempt to explain because, as one leading doctor of chemistry said, 'There is no point in me trying it because I know it cannot work.' Yet, the weird thing is that it not only works, but it's also damn easy to prove that it works. The snag is that you do not get those nice, neat and easy results, which you get from experiments in science lessons. Remember that nature is cyclic and the moon influences the tides, so it is highly likely that these natural forces also influence your divination.

CHAPTER 14

RITES DE PASSAGE AND RITUAL SEX

The transition from one phase of life or social status to another marks an important stage in physical, social or religious development. Such transitions are often accompanied by a ceremony or ritual, particularly in primitive societies, and although these rites are also evident in civilised societies, they are often modified to accommodate a conservative and conventional outlook. Such rites are known as rites de passage and they are generally defined as rites that accompany every change of place, state or social position. Birth, puberty, marriage and death are obvious rites de passage but also included are such transitions as a tribe or country going to war, entry into a secret society or religious group and graduation from a university. All are celebrated with some kind of ceremony or rite.

Initiation into the mysteries, a symbolic rebirth, is also a rite de passage. It implies the development of a higher level of consciousness, often achieved after passing through a number of grades or degrees; this allows certain laws of the universe, which are hidden from the layman, to be imparted to the initiate in accordance with the grade. True initiation is the direct influencing of the still immature consciousness of a pupil by the evolved spiritual consciousness of the teacher.

Because initiation is a symbolic rebirth, it is often conducted in the nude and this is exemplified today in the case of the Old Religion that, in essence, is a mystery religion. It is regrettable that the concept of nudity, even ritual nudity, appears to be so distasteful and even dirty to a large proportion of a generally inhibited western civilisation. Much of this attitude stems from previous teaching, particularly that of the Church, which had good reason

The five-fold kiss being performed during an initiation with the High Priestess and the Hand Maiden helping the newcomer to join the coven.

to discourage anything with a sexual connotation because of its magical implication. Many Gardnerian and Alexandrian covens normally work in the nude, or 'sky clad' as it is known, but true Traditional covens are robed except for initiation, which is always in the nude.

There are very good reasons for nude initiations and it is certainly not limited to the Old Religion. To show that nudity was also partaken by the Hebrew prophets, Janet and Stewart Farrar, in *The Witches Bible*, quote 1 Samuel, (Kings) XXI, 24:

And he stripped himself also of his garments,
and prophesied with the rest before Samuel, and
lay down naked all that day and night. Wherefore
they say, is Saul also among the prophets?

Sex is, among many other attributes, a magical experience and a magical technique that endows those who participate with certain powers not normally available. The Church would never condone such powers being usurped by ordinary men and women. It is because of these magical powers that sex has played such an important role in higher initiation. Because of the magical aspect of sex, nakedness was often taboo and sex was implied by a veiled woman. The sight of the naked Diana killed Actaeon and the sight of the naked Athena blinded Tiresias. The sight of a naked woman was only permitted in the higher Tantric initiations and in the higher initiations of the Greek mysteries.

Complete nakedness represents the state of absolute and simple being, but this state is only attainable after initiation into the mysteries. The sacred dance of the seven veils is symbolic and expressive of passing through the seven planetary spheres and freeing oneself, in stages, of the various inhibitions, feelings of guilt and conditioning qualities associated with those spheres. These qualities were thought of as being jewellery, ornaments and clothes that were to be thrown away successively until the state of ultimate nakedness was reached. This is expressed again in the case of Ishtar, the Mesopotamian goddess of love and fertility, when she descended into the underworld. Ereshkigal, the queen of the underworld, ordered the gatekeeper to deal with Ishtar in accordance with the age-old lore which required the Goddess to be stripped of her jewellery and finally her clothes as she passed through the seven gates of the underworld. She was then brought naked before Ereshkigal who ordered her to be sprinkled with the water of life before being escorted from the underworld to restore fertility to the land.

In a number of societies, sexual ritual has been used to manifest the presence of a god or goddess in order that a group or an individual could receive this being. This was the reason for the practice of sacred prostitution in the temples of the Mediterranean Aphrodite pantheon, Aphrodite, Ishtar, Innini and Mylitta. The priestesses were specifically linked to these temples for the service of the Goddess and the rituals celebrated were intended to invoke the divine female principle so that her presence in the community could be revived and nurtured. They celebrated sex as a magical rite which fostered the power and mystery associated with the Goddess when she had been invoked; they allowed their male sexual partners to receive the influence and virtues of the Goddess. The priestesses were known as virgins, pure ones or blessed ones.

There was also another aspect of this practice. Every girl, on reaching puberty, had to give up her virginity in a sacred sexual ritual before she could be married. Her partner would be any stranger who made a symbolic offering and invoked, through her, the Great Goddess.

The ritual sex role of woman was not limited to the Mediterranean Greek goddesses. In the Indian temples, where Vishna was venerated, the ritual offering of virgins was deemed to arouse and manifest the presence of the divinity. Temple dancers, in their role of priestesses, performed the same duties as the Greek and Mesopotamian priestesses of Aphrodite and Ishtar. The dances were generally performed with many evocatory gestures known as mudra while Asana described special magical positions of the body. All the temple priestesses were thoroughly trained in these techniques. Sexual practices for mystical purposes are also found in Taoist teachings, the orgiastic rites found in the Persian-Arab region and among some esoteric Christian groups. In all these rites of the mystery religions, the woman plays a leading and active role; this is particularly evident in some of the Tantric techniques in which the active role of the woman allows the man to exercise a special concentration of his mind. This is in stark contrast to male dominated western civilisation where she all too often plays a passive, submissive and subservient role.

Ritual sex was the method for man and woman to participate in the sacrum (the raising of magical energy). This was a technique used to experience contact with divinity and to receive the Goddess. This, of course, is the true purpose of the Great Rite but, as far as I know, this is not mentioned in books or, indeed, in covens practising the Great Rite. It is certainly made quite clear in the teaching of Traditional Witchcraft, the Old Religion.

Witches are closely associated with the moon through a moon goddess but originally the deity associated with the moon was a god who represented the moon as a fertility influence and whose earthly emissary was the king. Mene was a Phrygian moon god, Osiris an Egyptian moon god and Sin, another moon god, was the ancient lawgiver. Moses received the Tablets of the Law on Mount Sinai, the mountain of the moon.

In ancient religions, where the Moon God was worshipped, women worshippers and the king or headman representing the Moon God took part in a marriage ceremony and slept together as part of the celebrations. This was a hieros gamos, a sacred marriage, and was essential to ensure the fertility of the women and also of the crops and herds. Ceremonies like this were an important part of the annual celebrations associated with the moon; during the festivities which followed, women showed an abandon which may have been totally foreign to their normal behaviour. These were rites to honour a god of fertility and it was considered a duty to engage in lascivious activity in order to please the moon god and to stimulate his fertilising powers by taking part in sensuous and lustful merry making. This would ensure that the God bestowed his fertilising powers on the tribe and their activities.

Because of the important role women played in these celebrations, and because the twenty-eight-day cycle of the moon closely agreed with the menstrual cycle of women, the Moon God was replaced by a goddess; in Mesopotamia, for instance, Sin was replaced by Ishtar. Temples to the Moon Goddess began to emerge, particularly in the Middle East, and the scene was set for her worship in many parts of the world under many different names: Cybele in Phrygia, Anahita in Persia, Demeter in Greece or Ceres in Rome, and Artemis in Greece or Diana in Rome. All of these were worshipped as the Great Mother Goddess for many centuries before the coming of Christ.

In his superb book, *The Metaphysics of Sex,* Julius Evola concludes, 'Sex is the greatest magical force in nature; an impulse acts in it which suggests the mystery of the One, even when almost everything in the relationship between man and woman deteriorates into animal embraces and is exhausted and dispersed in a faded idealising sentimentality or in the habitual routine of socially acceptable conjugal relations.'

The Church is fully aware of the magical aspects of sex and this is one of the reasons why it is so insistent on stressing that sex is solely for the procreation of children and is a sin if practised for any other reason. The temples, lodges and covens, realising the power latent within the sexual process, very carefully guard certain techniques that they teach. Renegade members of esoteric societies have made some of these techniques public and it is possible to encounter some by pure chance. However, the power available is such that it could be devastating if encountered by those who are untrained to handle such power.

Many people, quite outside any magical ritual, have experienced strange phenomena during the build up to a sexual experience. These phenomena are not simply subjective. The most convincing manifestation of this psychic energy is the 'psychic report', a sharp bang which occurs somewhere in the general vicinity. The report is caused by the dissipation of psychic energy and is certainly not subjective since others can also hear it. The writer knows of a case where people in the street, two stories below, looked up to the window where a psychic report manifested.

Our ultimate goal is to achieve reunion with the Creative Principle in which there is perfect balance: neither male nor female, but the potential of either or both. Perfect balance does not exist on the physical plane where we find polarisation into positive and negative, light and dark and male and female. Only the seed is present and this manifests in humans as the animus and anima of Jungian psychology, the hidden element of the opposite sex within the psyche. This idea of the seed of the positive occurring in the negative and vice versa can be seen again in the symbol of Yin and Yang.

It can be clearly seen that this seed does not balance the dominant element, and to achieve this balance, the key to the mysteries, it is necessary to bring together the male and female in complete harmony. Balance and harmony are represented in the Old Religion by the High Priestess and the High Priest and by working partners of the opposite sex. Further evidence is provided by admission into the Circle and initiation being conducted by the opposite sex. The culmination of the complete harmonious interaction of the opposite poles is achieved in an initiation rite involving ritual sex; a magical celebration that should involve the physical, mental and spiritual levels. In Gardnerian Wicca and its derivatives, this is also known as the Great Rite and it takes place during initiation into the third degree. The rite can be 'actual', involving intercourse between the initiator and the initiate, or 'symbolic' where the athame represents the male principle and the chalice the female principle. The insertion of the athame into the chalice is symbolic of sexual union. In Traditional Witchcraft, initiations, with their associated magical celebrations, involve symbolic transitions through the elements from earth to spirit, each a 'rite de passage'. Ritual sex may sometimes accompany initiation into the last three elements of air, fire and spirit.

In Western civilisation we are too often firmly chained to the rock of fear, convention and guilt, and to the dictum of 'thou shalt not'. This leads to the inhibition of our basic instincts causing disturbed energy patterns that create stress with all its dire consequences. We can live a stress-free life if we listen to our unconscious mind and abide by what it is telling us. The unconscious mind knows what we need, and clearly tells us, but the conscious mind often overrules it because of the 'thou shalt not' syndrome. This is particularly evident in the case of the sex drive: a potent force which psychologists tell us is motivated by the need for the propagation of the species. Occult science teaches that sexual excitation enhances extrasensory perception and opens a door to the unconscious mind and thus the astral plane, and that this optimises during orgasm. As Dr Jonn Mumford says in *Sexual Occultism*, 'sex magic rests upon the fact that the most important psycho-physiological event in the life of a human being is an orgasm.'

Life in the modern world proceeds at such a pace that psychic tension is built up and, as mentioned earlier, this can be released spontaneously as a psychic report during sexual excitement. If the nervous energy generated is not dissipated, but is permitted to accumulate, mental problems can result. Sexual activity is the perfect natural tranquilliser, allowing the balance of the nervous system to be restored. The sabbats, which are associated with turning points in the Wheel of the Year, are festivals appropriately symbolising these times, but they are also feast days and joyous occasions. They finish up with games, which like the old times mentioned in an earlier chapter, may have a sexual connotation. With the building up of power during the ritual, and the general excitement of the occasion, no member of the Old Religion would ever deny that the games occasionally get very lively as they can in any party.

If, on the other hand, sexual desire is repressed because it is considered to be a sin or something dirty, it may be hidden in the unconscious mind. If this perfectly natural desire is too strong to resist, the situation may result in a feeling of guilt. This can then be expelled from consciousness and pushed even deeper into the unconscious from where it cannot be recalled at will, resulting in a repressed complex with dire consequences for health.

The Old Religion has never looked upon sexual activity as a sin in the way that the Church does. Sex is regarded as a perfectly natural activity, which should be enjoyed without shame or guilt, as a gift from the Creator.

CHAPTER 15

LIVING THE WAY
OF A WITCH

Whether you are accepted as a neophyte in a Traditional coven depends, to a very large extent, on your attitude to life, the way you relate to your fellow beings and the environment, and the way you conduct yourself in order to play a full role in the process of life. Traditional Witchcraft should not be something that concerns you only at the esbats and sabbats; the Old Religion should concern the whole of you the whole of the time. You should always be ready to help anyone who requires help, whatever his or her faith or creed.

From the time of your first initiation into the Old Religion, you should be keeping what Gardnerians and many offshoots call a *Book of Shadows*, but Traditionals call *The Book*. *The Book* is a comparatively recent concept, not a relic of the past. Obviously the kind of material that should constitute *The Book* would, during the persecution, have been concrete evidence of association with a coven, which would have resulted in dire punishment. Many Gardnerians and Alexandrians that I have met believed that the *Book of Shadows* does have an ancient origin and have even said that the original is in the British Library! This is probably because the rather sinister title, conferred on it by Gerald Gardner, does tend to conjure up such a belief. In fact, *The Book* of the Traditionals originated early in the twentieth century merely to enhance the teaching of the Old Religion, which had always been handed down 'from mouth to ear'.

Rituals performed during sabbats, together with any you have composed, should be recorded in *The Book*. Composing a ritual for a sabbat promotes greater insight into the true meaning of the sabbat and encourages a far deeper

Above and right: The Book or the *Book of Shadows* can either be handwritten or a file containing loose leaves of notes. There is nothing unusual about this and in many ways it is like a good cookery recipe book – containing all sorts of useful information for future reference.

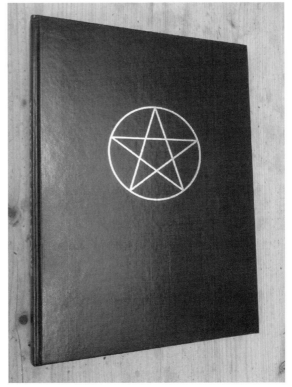

157

rapport with nature. *The Book* should be a comprehensive manual of the teaching and philosophy of the Old Religion and should include everything that will allow you to live in greater rapport with the universal tides and the forces of nature. You must be prepared to look at the iceberg below the water as well as the tip above. You should include the correspondences for colour, incense, perfume etc for every day of the week and you should use them. The planet Mercury, for example, governs Wednesday, so candles should be yellow, perfume Lavender, incense Cinnamon and oil Lavender or Lemongrass. Notes on such topics as healing, herbal lore and spells for suitable purposes should be included.

An ideal Book would be one consisting of loose-leaf inserts which enable you to add new information in the appropriate place. It is better if the binder and inserts are A4 size and, of course, you should use recycled paper or paper made from sustainable sources. You may wish to cover the binder or decorate it with symbols appropriate to the Craft or you may wish to have a totally innocuous cover. There are good arguments for and against.

Because the sabbats are important occasions, marking different phases in the Wheel of the Year, they should, unless there is a very good reason for absence, be celebrated with the coven. If it is impossible to attend the sabbat with the coven, the High Priestess or the High Priest should be informed and an appropriate ritual should be celebrated at home. Similarly, esbats should be attended because it is during these that the teaching takes place.

Throughout this book I have alluded to a universal force, which pervades the whole of nature and can, under certain circumstances and using certain techniques, be 'tapped into'. It is axiomatic of the teaching of the Old Religion that the physical Universe is only a part of total reality. The fact is that we exist as physical beings on the physical plane and in order to work magic, the universal force must function via the physical body. Consequently, it is essential to keep the body fit and healthy. Because stray elementals can 'lock onto' dirt and stale body fluids, it is also vital to be scrupulously clean when engaged in any magical operation.

Health and fitness are not synonymous terms; health depends largely on personal habits and a positive psychological attitude, fitness depends primarily on the efficiency of the muscular and cardio-respiratory systems. The extent of the efficiency will be related to the amount and quality of exercise undertaken and this, in turn, requires will and determination, both psychological qualities.

According to the French philosopher, Rene Descartes (1596-1650), the body is governed by mechanical laws but the mind, or soul, is free and immortal. This was characteristic of Descartes' philosophy, the division of complex systems into their constituent parts in order to understand them. This reasoning has been responsible for medicine, in general, ignoring a psychological aspect of disease and, in consequence, treating the symptoms but not the cause. Modern physics has done much to prevent the fundamental error of treating the whole as the sum of the parts. With the exception of the absolute diehards, it is now generally accepted that the consciousness of the experimenter can influence the outcome of an experiment, so consciousness can also affect all aspects of life. This is an important point to be considered during magical operations.

In the late 1920s, the English physicist Paul Dirac suggested that only fields are real in the universe; matter is but a momentary manifestation of inter-acting fields. A field is a region in which force is experienced, therefore mankind and the universe can be thought of as a collection of interacting forces and the world 'out there' is simply illusion, the Maya of the Hindus. There is no absolute reality. What we perceive and what becomes reality to us has resulted due to an interaction between us and what we observe; the 'reality' will thus be conditioned by our psychological make-up. Eastern religion has always accepted this line of thought. Laama Anagarika, a Tantric Buddhist, says:

> The Buddhist does not believe in an independent or separately existing external world, into whose dynamic forces he could insert himself. The external world and his inner world are for him only two sides of the same fabric in which the threads of all forces and all events, of all forms of consciousness and of their objects, are woven into an inseparable net of endless, mutually conditioned relations.

This universal interaction can have a profound effect on a person's health, mental and physical. The fundamental inter-dependence between body and mind, and its importance in general health, has always been accepted by eastern mystics, the shamans and many esoteric groups, but it is only on the fringes of acceptance by western orthodox medicine. Since Descartes postulated the strict separation of body and mind, medicine has tended to leave the health of the body to the physician and the health of the mind to the psychiatrist.

It is only in comparatively recent times that orthodox medicine has linked malfunction of the body with psychological disturbance and recognised psychogenic pain and psychosomatic illness. There appears to be a link between body and mind in an increasing number of illnesses and we may yet discover that all disease has its origin in the realm of mind or spirit. The shaman considers that all illness is the consequence of some disharmony with the cosmic order and uses such therapeutic techniques as dream analysis, psychodrama and guided imagery, all of which are practised in the Old Religion and prescribed in psychotherapy today.

Keeping yourself healthy requires you to adopt a positive attitude of mind towards good health, to exercise regularly and to eat sensibly. The value of 'positive thought' is based on the fundamental inter-dependence between mind and body. There is an adage that should be kept constantly in mind by those who seek the 'golden key' to a happy and fruitful life:

As a person thinketh, so is he.

A positive attitude to life gives rise to an outflow of energy, which appears to affect other living organisms. Dr Grad of McGill University in Montreal found that water from a sealed flask, which a healer had held, significantly increased the growth of plants treated with it. However, water in a flask held by a depressive retarded seeds and plants from the same batch. This gives a clue to the draining of energy one feels when in the presence of a so-called psychic vampire. Most of us have, at some time or other, encountered such a person. It is best to avoid them, but protection can be assured by vividly visualising yourself surrounded by a brilliant electric blue sphere.

Any information acquired by psychic means has to be brought into consciousness to be acted upon; to be of any avail on the physical plane, the plane upon which we exist as incarnate beings, action has to take place via the physical body. Even if the action requires further psychic means to achieve a result in, for instance, a spell or healing, a decision first has to be made in the conscious state before being activated on the psychic plane via the unconscious mind. It is therefore highly desirable, if not essential, for the physical body to be in a good state of health and fitness. As I have mentioned, it is of prime importance to develop a positive attitude to health, but it is also necessary to exercise regularly. The well-known saying 'use or lose' is very apt. The muscles, for example, can atrophy if not used and muscular activity assists the venous return of blood to the heart, which, of course, is also a muscle. All the systems of the body require a supply of blood to provide them with oxygen and food and to carry away waste products.

Dancing formed an important event at many witchcraft meetings, but photographing such movement in Bill's small and dimly lit room was most difficult.

The development and maintenance of physical fitness necessitates the use of exercise for the whole body and this exercise can be broadly divided into three types: mobility exercises, strength exercises and cardio-respiratory exercises.

Mobility exercises are concerned with the movement of muscles and joints through the complete range. It may be that joint mobility has already been reduced by constant use of the joint through a limited range that may have been caused by a sedentary occupation without leisure-time exercise. Lack of mobility in joints is often found in desk-bound people making it difficult for them to lead an active life. Dancing round the Circle during the opening and closing rituals of the Old Religion is certainly active and this is one of many reasons why witches should keep themselves fit. Mobility of the joints can be restored to a great extent, and further loss prevented, by the correct use of exercise. With correct use of exercise a desirable freedom and grace of movement will always be retained, but it is essential that advice on exercise should be sought from a qualified and competent teacher.

Unless you wish to become a body-builder, the development of excessive muscle bulk is unnecessary. The acquisition of muscular strength should not

Everyday activities for many witchcraft covens include the so-called nature walk, a stroll through the countryside along well worn footpaths simply to enjoy the presence of nature and perhaps make some interesting discoveries along the way. Many modern Scout groups like the one pictured here include such walks in their programmes, so exploring nature is not unique to witches. A large number of town dwellers also enjoy the countryside and many of them go to considerable lengths to enjoy the isolation, serenity and bounty that the natural world has to offer. These days there are a vast number of excellent guide books to help with the identification of all sorts, and it is always useful to have a guide handy which will help to identify or confirm what you have found.

be regarded as an end in itself; it is a means to be applied to other ends such as making you more efficient in lifting and carrying heavy things. The use of weights makes the development of strength very easy to control and is to be highly recommended. A lot of fast movement with manageable weights is much better than using heavy weights with slower movements unless, as I said before, you wish to become a body-builder.

The heart is composed of a specialised muscular tissue, which responds to exercise by increasing its efficiency. The heart thrives on activity and is adversely affected by inactivity. This is a very good reason for people in sedentary occupations to engage in some form of sustained, energetic activity. When sustained exercise is taken, the muscles require more oxygen so the heart is called upon to increase the rate and power of the beat in order to supply the extra blood necessary to provide this increase in oxygen.

The best and safest exercises for the heart are the endurance type involving the large, bulky muscles of the thighs and abdomen. The rhythmic and repetitive movements of these large muscles have a definite massaging effect on the blood vessels. The return of venous blood to the heart is thus greatly assisted. Examples of the type of exercise required in this group are squats, running, stepping on and off a stool, cycling, rowing and skipping.

The efficiency of the cardio-respiratory system can be ascertained by the time taken for the pulse to return to its normal rate following severe exertion. You can, and should, check this for yourself by taking your resting pulse rate and then stepping on and off a stool for about fifteen seconds or until you feel your heart beating faster than usual. You should keep a record of the time the pulse takes to return to normal. Trained people have a slower pulse rate and a shorter recovery time than untrained people. A little exercise often is better than a lot of exercise taken once a week.

Eating sensibly means a whole food diet, low in sugar, salt and fat and high in fibre, vitamins and minerals, with plenty of fresh fruit and vegetables, which have preferably been grown organically. Substances of various kinds are added to food for a number of reasons but many additives have a detrimental effect on health. Since the beginning of 1986, all foods have to specify the additives in the list of ingredients, by name or E number, and also the purpose of the additive. Fruit and vegetables may have been grown in chemically adulterated soil or have been sprayed with chemical pest control agents so those who practise the Old Religion should be wise enough to carefully check the list of ingredients before purchasing and to insist on organically grown produce if finances allow.

Everyone knows about the off-days of life or has heard someone say 'it's not my day today' but how many realise that we are profoundly influenced by natural cycles? Those of the Old Path know that life is affected by cosmic tides that give rise to rhythmic patterns in all living organisms; a knowledge of these rhythms enables us to progress through life on favourable tides. Some of these tides and cycles are particularly important in magic but all of them constantly affect our lives.

Certain customs and rites have been built around the equinoxes and the solstices but they also mark the seasonal tides: the Tide of Destruction, Tide of Sowing, Tide of Reaping and Tide of Planning. The Old Religion attaches great importance to these tides but they are also beautifully expressed in Ecclesiastes 3 (i):

> To every thing there is a season, and a time to every purpose under the heaven: a time to be born, and a time to die; a time to plant, and a time to pluck up that which is planted.

Of all the heavenly bodies, the moon is the closest to earth; because of its proximity, it has a profound effect on all living organisms and on the planet. The most obvious effect is the gravitational force causing the tides. Hans Horbiger, an Austrian engineer, once proposed a theory that the earth has had more than one moon. Each of the moons, in turn, approached closer and closer to Earth, and as it did so, gravitation increased causing a race of giants and great floods – both in accord with folklore and mythology.

The lunar tides are very important in all magical work; practical magic should never be attempted during a waning moon. In the Old Religion the Moon Goddess plays an important role in all the rites and the waxing moon, full moon and waning moon are symbolised by the Maid, Mother and Crone respectively. It should be carefully noted that the three phases of the moon are 'a time for' and every endeavour should be made to abide by this in everyday life. The waxing moon is a time for expansion, growth and invoking; the full moon is a time for fulfilment, stability and reaping; and the waning moon is a time for reducing activity, for rest and reflection.

Time is one of life's biggest bugbears. It is the easiest thing in the world to say, and believe, 'I haven't got time' or 'I will do it tomorrow'. No more time will be found tomorrow than today. Do it now! There is no time like the present is a well-known saying, but those who follow the Old Path know, as mentioned in an earlier chapter, that the present only exists within the conscious mind. However, in our incarnate state, we function, to a large extent, in the conscious mind and time does have to be considered. During incarnation, time is a precious commodity that should not be frittered away. Time must be found for regular exercise and for topics such as meditation which will help you to progress along the Path. Time must always be found for the esbats and the sabbats. There really is no time like the present time and time must be found to do today what you are thinking of putting off until tomorrow.

PART FOUR

LIFE AND DEATH
IN
WITCHCRAFT

CHAPTER 16

THE CYCLE OF LIFE
BY TONI HUGHES

Do be sure to notice on your Tarot deck that the card of death is one of great change, when one phase of life ends and a new phase begins.

Our dear High Priest of the Sacred Coven of Ceridwen, Bill Love, died on 20 December 2011 aged just a few days short of 87 years. He had been troubled by ill health for over a year before his body succumbed to further weakness and then, finally, to death. Yet all this time his brain continued to function perfectly and his mind remained highly active until the very end. He still worked on this book only a few weeks before he died. Bill then passed through the ultimate initiation in this earthly incarnation to make the transition to the spiritual planes. His passing was quiet and peaceful. His funeral, however, was anything but peaceful or miserable. He wanted and got a cheerful event with people wearing bright colours and the service included a jazz band playing a rendition of the song *Lord of the Dance* for all to join in. Everybody present did their best to sing in tune and to give it some of the gusto with which Bill had lived all his life. This celebration of Bill's life also included a reading from Kahil Gibran's book *The Prophet* on what it is to die and concluded with the beautiful, evocative verses of *The Charge of the Star Goddess* by Doreen Valiente, who is known by many as the Mother of modern Witchcraft. Following this brief service, two majestic white horses pulled a simple cart bearing Bill in his wicker coffin. They clip-clopped through the tree-lined walkway of the cemetery past the sea of headstones to a new virgin area set aside as a natural meadow. The horses were resplendent with yellow plumes adorning their heads. This colour was

Bill asked for a an eco-friendly or 'green' funeral and therefore had a basket-like coffin made from sustainable natural materials. This was taken to its final place of rest on a simple carriage pulled by two horses. Bill was the first person to be laid to rest on a new piece of land set aside for natural burials. In spring and summer this piece of land becomes a flowery meadow with trees providing shelter and homes for birds and other animals.

especially chosen, in the way of the Old Religion, to represent the colour of the day, Wednesday. Bill's many friends and family members were milling around silently, gazing upon the horses and the coffin as they passed by. The atmosphere was one of reverence and awe at such a magnificent, yet simple sight.

At the time not many knew that Bill, looking every inch the witch and magician that he had been, was buried in his brown robe, as is the way of Traditional Witchcraft. He held his Tarot deck in one hand and his set of runes in the other as his body was returned to the Goddess whence he had come, and the natural grassland grave was covered with earth, the element through which he had taken his first steps into the Old Religion.

'Oh Great Goddess and Great God, we ask you to be here with us so that you may receive the body of our much loved High Priest, Bill. He who has passed through the final initiation of this earthly incarnation and who has experienced the dissolution of his body shall now be with you. He shall float in the loving warmth of the Goddess' womb until the time arrives when he shall be ready to enter the mystery of the Cauldron of Rebirth. Bill has fulfilled the reason for this life on earth; he has experienced much and has passed his knowledge on to those who follow him. His purpose is done; his lessons are learnt. Now his soul must travel on, evolving in strength, wisdom and spirituality. The cycle of life, death and rebirth continuing as it has since the beginning of time.'

And witches say, 'Merry meet, merry part and merry meet again.'

It is not just Pagans who are opting for what is now known as natural or eco-friendly funerals. These 'green' burials uphold the concept of using biodegradable materials for the coffin such as bamboo, willow or even re-cycled cardboard, to ensure that harmful chemicals are not put into the ground. At the same time this negates the polluting effects of the traditional varnished hardwood, chipboard or other modern material coffins, and it does not incur the destruction of any trees.

The burial ground is allowed to return to nature, which then aids plant growth and encourages wildlife. This concept seems to have been grasped by the Norsemen long before the lifeless English cemeteries were created. All around the Baltic one will find a large number of centres where the dead are surrounded by the most amazing wild life, often far richer in rare species than nearby nature reserves.

Bill's Pagan faith helped him to form the firm belief that death is a normal part of the natural cycle of life: the birth, death and rebirth continuum. He often told me that he was absolutely certain the soul lives on. There are many examples of this cycle of continuum in Witchcraft circles and some are found within the sabbats or ancient Celtic festivals, which were mentioned earlier.

If we start on the sabbat wheel at Samhain, we can see that it marks both endings and beginnings. This is particularly so when we consider that all vegetation on earth is dying and that the Goddess and the God are in the underworld. Yet in the midst of this darkness the old Celtic New Year commences, bringing with it new hope of life to come.

This affirmation of new life is confirmed at the Winter Solstice when the sun is born anew, caressing the earth with warmth and with the thought of a fresh cycle of growth.

At Imbolg, the Triple Goddess had transformed from her crone aspect into her maiden or virgin aspect and thus the earth is reawakened with its potential for growth everywhere.

The Spring Equinox finds the phallic Horned God impregnating the Spring Maiden Goddess and that all of nature is fertile with the initial growth of vegetation well under way.

At Beltane the marriage of the Spring Maiden and the Horned God produce an abundance of energy associated with wild rampant vegetative growth.

Thereafter, the Summer Solstice sees life at its peak of potency and manifestation. The Mother Goddess asks the God to help her in caring for the land and he, therefore, assumes his responsibilities.

Furthermore, we see the result of the Goddess' work culminating in the production of fruit and seeds, which contain the new life for the next year. Then there is a downward turn towards death.

At Lughnasadh, the first harvest, the Goddess in her crone phase strikes down the Sun God, who is in his aspect of the sacrificial corn king, so that through his death, life shall be eventually renewed. He is now in the underworld.

The Autumn Equinox is the twilight of the year and the God decides to briefly return from the underworld in order to take the Goddess back with him.

With both Crone Goddess and the Sun God in the underworld, the earth becomes barren and vegetation re-enters the dark womb of the Mother Goddess in readiness for regeneration or rebirth.

Thus it is seen that the cycle of life, death and rebirth, through the seasons, may be symbolised by the interactions of the Goddess and of the God through the old Celtic Pagan festivals.

A shield with the Green Man by the side of a modern door.

Inspiration for the cycle of life can also be found when one starts delving into Nordic folk festivals and looks at the history of the Green Man. He embodies the life cycle in his vegetation aspect where we learn that his seed of potential grows into a strong, upright shoot, which then flowers and sends seeds into the earth before it dies again. The Green Man is then reborn from the depths of Mother Earth for the cycle to repeat itself the following year.

For a Pagan there is a wealth of the life/death cycle or the life in death symbology. For example:

- Evergreen trees and plants are viewed as a life in death symbol.
- Mistletoe is a symbol of immortality.
- The snake or serpent represents rebirth due to it shedding of the skin.
- The butterfly has a metamorphic life cycle symbolising transformation and the mystical rebirth of the soul.
- The corn dolly encompasses the spirit of the corn until spring when it will again be needed at the heart of the next crops growths.
- The moon undergoes a never-ending process of death and rebirth in its twenty-eight-day cycle, thus it symbolises the rhythms of life and death.
- The wheel symbolises the earthly cycles of renewal and reincarnation.

Corn dollies can look most simple, but trying to work out how they are made can be difficult if there is no one around to show how it is done.

- The cauldron is an archetypal symbol of transformation, i.e. sacrifices, death and rebirth. It was often thought that any dead thrown into the cauldron were reborn the next day.
- The spiral represents the cycle of life. The triskele or triskelion is the Celtic triple spiral symbol for the power of life and rebirth.

This life cycle is so well ingrained in the psyche of one from the Old Religion, through ritual and the sabbats, that death should not hold so much fear as it may for a person from other religious persuasions. The witch learns to live close to the earth and is aware of its transformations and the birth, life, death and rebirth cycles of nature. This cycle brings about all manifestation as well as the natural order of the universe. We are on a line of continuum always and pass through the same veil when we die as we do when we are reborn. After the death of the body, the soul gradually reaches perfection as it goes through the many lives of reincarnation and in time learns the lessons needed during each incarnation to achieve this goal.

The soul energy, the essential *you*, lives on after the death of the physical body and is not, any longer, bound by the needs of the flesh. Some Pagans believe that the personality remains in the soul energy and that this is not changed by death. What a person can do in life, he can also do in death and it may even be enhanced, as he is then pure consciousness. However, the soul also has a Higher Self, which eventually absorbs the personality after which it is conditioned for its next incarnation.

The soul can be thought of as all energy, without gender and without form. Even the laws of physics tell us that energy cannot be destroyed and that it can only be transformed. The soul remains in the birth/life/death/rebirth cycle and the decomposing body provides sustenance for another life form.

So where does the soul go when the body dies? The Old Religion mentions the Celtic Summerland and Avalon, which is also known as the Isle of Apples and can be found somewhere in the mists towards the south-west of ancient Britain. The Irish call it the Land of Youth or Tir Na N'og.

It matters not what the place of rest and recuperation is called, for all souls will find themselves at the level of the spiritual realms that is right for them. It appears that there are two main types of soul: those who will be impelled to reincarnate again and those who will advance to the higher spiritual realms, choosing either to remain there or to incarnate by choice.

This latter type of soul has achieved the ultimate realisation and can be considered as *freed*. In terms of the Old Religion, the freed soul dwells with the Goddess and the God in the higher realms. This is the advanced soul, which is concerned with humanity's well-being and evolution.

In occult circles it is thought that the soul goes to the astral plane or the spiritual realms. The soul's plane, or Summerland, is much less dense than the physical plane and operates at an extremely high frequency. For communication to happen with a soul, the lower frequency of a person has to be raised to a much higher degree. One who has the intense occult or magical training may be able to accomplish this, but it is usually rather difficult, so a soul will sometimes get in touch through a person's dreams.

The souls that are reached by a clairvoyant or psychic are those that remain in the lower levels of the astral and are on the path of reincarnation. They may still feel attachment to loved ones, have unfinished business or simply a need to let those closest to them know that their soul lives on. The psychic should not attempt to communicate with the more advanced souls who have passed beyond the wheel of reincarnation, as these souls have a much higher and wider remit of looking out for humanity as a whole.

The nature of the soul is an intriguing subject which can be discussed indefinitely, however, this could make a book for itself so, at this point, the subject of the soul shall be left to rest in peace.

So what sort of indications are there that may lead us to a belief in the continuance of the soul and in reincarnation? There are many pointers to an afterlife and beyond. For example:

- Personal experience: this may take the form of feeling the presence of the deceased in various ways. After Bill had died, for approximately eighteen hours he enveloped me in energy, which can only be described as love. In the succeeding days and weeks I felt his energy and presence very strongly. The energy would course through my entire being. I also saw many elementals, up to a month after his death, which I associated with Bill. Finally, he sent a message through a couple of dreams, telling me that he was going away. Thereafter, Bill did become a lot more distant, but intermittently I can still feel his presence, even after a few months. As I write, Bill has not yet reincarnated. Bill was an accomplished occultist as well as a witch and being able to do all of the above, in life anyway, he would certainly be able to manage it all in death.

- NDEs (Near Death Experiences): when a person dies and is brought back to life, it is sometimes found that they have undergone an extreme spiritual experience whilst dead. Commonly, they may astraly project and view their body from a distance before being propelled through a dark tunnel towards brilliant white light. Sometimes they meet loved ones or a Supreme Being and feel an all-consuming love. After returning to their body, the person's character may be completely changed for the better, and they often have a new outlook on life.

- Hypnotic regression: when a hypnotist regresses a person to an early stage of their life, then that person may recall a past life or lives before being born. Confirmation of these lives can result from research into the information extracted. (However, this a most misunderstood process and too many regressions stop when some evidence of a past life is uncovered. The hypnotic sessions should continue far beyond the stage when the regression appears because in many cases this will also reveal the sources of the information. It is also important that the hypnotist doesn't implant the memories in his patient, as has been done unwittingly by too many.)

- Spiritualism: a belief whereby the spirit of a dead person may communicate through a medium. Care must be taken to filter out the fake mediums from the genuine ones.

- Dreams: after falling asleep, a person functions on the astral level and may dream about another life he has lived. They may even dream repetitively about the same life. Such dreams should always be recorded immediately upon waking and the details of the life can be confirmed through research.

- Ghosts, manifestations, EVP (Electronic Voice Phenomena) etc.: these are all indicative of the afterlife. EVP is the recording of spirit voices on a background of white noise.

- Science: modern quantum mechanics (the study of the atom's building blocks) tends to support the theory of an afterlife. Science is taking great strides towards realms that could support the idea of the existence of the soul.

- The Scole Report: during the 1990s at Scole in Norfolk three experienced investigators from the Society for Psychical Research (Montague Keen, Arthur Ellison and David Fontana) conducted an investigation into the Genuineness of a Range of Physical Phenomena associated with a Mediumistic Group in Norfolk (England). Some of the phenomena reported were: moving lights, manifestation of spirits and shapes, apports, electronic voice phenomena and the imposition of images on sealed films. Montague Keen concluded that fraud was not involved and that the phenomena were real.

There are many other indications of belief in the soul continuing and of reincarnation. It must be said that there is consistent evidence, although unproven, for the existence of the soul. In conclusion, all the religions of the world believe in life after death and most also in reincarnation, and that is something that should not be ignored.

CHAPTER 17

Searching for what Witchcraft can Offer

Natural Energy and Finding Answers

Anyone searching for specific answers to personal problems should steer well clear of living in harmony with nature or joining a coven because they are likely to find more and more questions rather than immediate solutions. In fact, there will be many occurrences where an explanation will never be forthcoming. Bill always emphasised the importance of searching for evidence; to take note of what is happening and to have time to absorb the information and feelings one comes across. This is important because such thought processes are totally different to what people are taught in schools. There the emphasis is on 'carefully thought out' answers, 'planning what you are going to write' before putting pen to paper and coming up with logical explanations. Bill put more emphasis on experience and building up a strong base of evidence or information.

What is Natural Energy?

Natural energy, the supernatural, what Bill called 'magic' or whatever you want to call it, is often treated with the gravest of suspicion. People tag it with mocking labels and many won't even listen to anyone who has experienced it. Others make it a subject of ridicule. So, the question one must ask is whether such energy and magic really exists, or whether it is imagined. This question can be answered by thinking about compasses. Can ships and aircraft really find their way with what is nothing more than a magnetised needle? What about thunderstorms? Are they real or are they figments of the imagination? Or tides? Do thousands of tons of water actually rise up all on their own against gravity? Many people are happy to believe in these natural phenomena, despite them sounding far more far-fetched than some other forms of more subtle natural energy.

Just think and ask yourself: have you ever experienced natural energy? Have you –

- felt strange electrifying air before a thunder storm?
- felt the difference in team spirit between losing and winning?
- ever taken an instant dislike to a person you have met for the first time?
- met someone for the first time and felt as if you had known him for ages?
- done something highly strenuous but still felt full of energy afterwards?
- done a small job and felt listless afterwards?
- felt drained of energy by another person who irritated you?
- met someone who made you feel full of energy?
- had the feeling of being watched, although you did not see anyone?
- sensed someone's presence before seeing, hearing or smelling them?
- anticipated an on-coming vehicle along an isolated country lane?
- thought of something or someone shortly before meeting them?
- felt threatened by others although no one said anything hostile?
- used a compass for navigating?
- had a feeling that there was something to do, but you didn't know what?
- been somewhere new, but found your way around easily?
- got lost in familiar surroundings?
- entered a room and felt uncomfortable?
- entered an empty room and felt as if you had walked into a bitter argument?
- felt uncomfortable during some weather conditions?
- noticed a strange feeling when entering someone's private room?
- met children who hate having their toys cleaned?
- ignored first gut feelings and later found that they were right?
- found some colours make you feel uncomfortable?
- sensed how other people were feeling although you didn't know them?

If you can say 'yes' to any of these, then you will have felt subtle forces of natural energy.

Modern Man's Phobia of Natural Energy

The majority of people are unaware of natural energy and the power it can contain because the leaders of mankind have always had the strong desire to produce a passive and obedient workforce. Their aim was to make the governing classes richer and stronger. Therefore access to free natural energy and healing power was discouraged. Workers were led to believe that only special officials with the appropriate training and wearing the right regalia can access this power. Yet people are continuously influenced by stimulation from deep inside their own subconscious and by energy or forces from outside their bodies. Unfortunately the vast majority just ignore this valuable aid and those that make use of it often find it is exceedingly difficult to determine whether the sensations come from within or from without.

The problem of sensing delicate outside energies is made worse by society, the churches, our way of life and the education system. All of these factors brainwash individuals to ignore outside influences. Children appear to be born with a natural ability to respond to outside stimuli, but quickly lose that skill. In addition to this, we are further weakened by the ticking clock syndrome. People who have a loudly ticking clock or live near another source of noise don't hear the disturbance because their brain automatically filters it out of their perception and they won't become aware of it until it stops. Sailors aboard ships, for example, often wake up when the noisy engines are turned off.

So we all have the uncanny ability of ignoring sounds, sights, smells, forces, vibrations and energies around us. This is rather practical because living in such an overpopulated society we would otherwise be overwhelmed by excess energies radiating around us every day, when were are surrounded by electricity, magnetic fields from motors and microwaves, static electricity from man-made materials, televisions, loads of people and the like.

One problem with learning how to use this energy and making use of one's own inert senses is that it is a little like becoming a stage magician. Everybody must have gaped with deep fascination at a convincing conjuring trick and then felt the anticlimax when they discovered how it was done. Magic suddenly turned into sour deceit and sorcery became a trick.

Exactly the same can happen when one joins a magical group or dabbles with natural energy. It is all too easy to marvel at the mysteries of nature and feel let down when one discovers the simplicity of the secret. It has been said before that many natural occurrences are indeed incredibly simple. So simple that one is sometimes left with the feeling of having been cheated, but this is the admirable feature of any journey of personal discovery: it is very, very simple. There is no need for complicated jargon, expensive scientific laboratories or long periods of study. Having said this, it is important to steer clear of anyone who claims to understand this simplicity. One certainty about people who claim they can provide definite answers for supernatural occurrences is that they have not yet seen the mountain and they definitely don't understand the problems. Those who know tend not to talk about it and those who talk tend not to know.

Pitfalls to Avoid

It is not necessary to join a coven in order to live in harmony with nature, however, anyone embarking upon such a path, especially if they have been brought up in an urban environment, must be aware of some common pitfalls when going it alone.

To start with, the Internet. This has not only revolutionised communications by making it possible to get in touch with people all over the globe, but it has also provided an even better misinformation system than television. Do be aware that there are a vast number of charlatans preying on vulnerable people and make sure those who demand high prices or impose inflammatory conditions for worthless services do not catch you out. Remember what Bill said earlier, you will never be asked to join a Traditional Witchcraft coven and the members won't ask you for money either. They often will be delighted if you were to bring some biscuits or nibbles to go with the drinks they provide, but they are not moneymakers.

The Internet has also helped to revolutionise the way we learn and a large number of brilliant home-study courses have become available at quite reasonable prices, but there are some things that cannot be learned from books or through the Internet. As Bill said earlier in this book, there are things that have got to be experienced. What is more, trying to get into some subjects requires a leader who has done it before and is still alive. For example, some sources mention that it is possible to make tea with birch and bramble leaves, but they failed to add that this can only be done while the leaves are still relatively young and that they will turn poisonous during summer months. This poison might not be strong enough to kill, but it could produce some quite appalling stomach pains. Even more astonishing is that some years ago there was an educational filmstrip about edible fungi with a photograph of a Destroying Angel on the first picture. This mushroom is deadly and people are beyond help once the symptoms show themselves.

There are some excellent diviners using a vast variety of media producing the most astonishing results, but do be aware of some characters at so called psychic fairs and ask yourself whether they are genuine or showmen. The adverts for some psychic fairs state that they are 'for entertainment only,' so one would expect the people there to wear fancy dress. Otherwise how would one know whether a person is a witch, Pagan, gypsy, belly dancer or whatever? Belonging to some unusual fringe society is important because the majority of people do not believe that straightforward, ordinary people wearing ordinary clothes can have psychic abilities.

Some aspects of what Bill called 'magic' have been taken over by serious science and now cover a wide variety of disciplines such as psychotherapy, hypnotherapy, physics, chemistry, biology, geology and the like. The astonishing things with these sciences is that they can be practiced without any scientific knowledge at all and you certainly don't have to learn any special technical words to understand some of the processes. The trouble with this is that it is also dead easy to make a hell of a mess without wanting to, and then find it difficult to get out of the disorder. For example, it is easy to learn how to hypnotise someone and to drop them into serious mental problems. Anyone studying clinical hypnotism, for example, will find that they spend more time learning about the workings of the brain and psychology than hypnosis. Damage and mental anguish caused by so-called stage hypnotists can be enormous, and there are practitioners in Harley Street who specialise in dealing with the victims of such charlatans. The trouble is that the average person cannot afford the high fees and could suffer for years of mental illness without knowing the cause of their trouble.

To give one example: Julia married in her mid-twenties and settled into a comfortable urban life, but before long she found that she had developed a powerful urge to kill her husband. She didn't have a history of violence and controlled herself, although that strong urge to murder her husband kept recurring. She had been listening to a self-hypnosis cassette. The idea was that you listened to the tape and then, at the end, while soft music continued to play, you kept telling yourself how you are going to change your life. The message she kept telling herself was, 'I will not chew my fingernails anymore.' Simple, but not effective, and with highly disastrous results. Neither the tape nor the instructions told her that the subconscious cannot calculate or reason.

It is highly likely that the message, which took hold in her subconscious was 'I will not bite anymore', and it was her husband who encouraged her to buy this tape. So every time she started eating, she found a powerful turmoil bubbling up inside her with a strong urge to get rid of the person who had created it. The message she should have given to herself is, 'I will enjoy watching my fingernails grow'. It is unlikely that such wording would produce serious side effects. Please don't imagine such influences as a passing fad. The results can be most serious and pain created by the imagination can be as agonizing as physical injuries. Julia got rid of the tape.

Anyone getting into serious meditation or into a deeply relaxed mental state should know that the subconscious cannot calculate or reason and it can't cope with negatives either. Whatever you think about must always be positive and it is important to play on the emotions rather than deal with facts. Facts don't mean a thing to your subconscious. In addition to stage hypnotists and well-meaning but destructive amateurs, there are also people who 'regress' others so that they can discover their past lives. This can be an exciting activity, but well-trained hypnotists know that what is happening is really half of a 'psychoanalysis or hypnoanalysis' and one needs to continue the process far beyond the point where the past life is discovered. When doing this, the person being regressed will later remember where the information from the 'past life' has come from and be considerably 'richer' as a result.

Dowsing is another skill anyone can learn exceedingly quickly. It is possible to teach someone to dowse in a matter of minutes, but one needs a lot of practice to do it properly. It is a little like learning to play the piano; once you know which keys to press, you need to practise to get it right and even then not everyone will become a concert pianist. Dowsing can be an exhausting activity. It tends to drain one of energy, therefore it is advisable to steer clear of people who manage to do it all day long. In any case, as has been said before, it is dead easy to swing pendulums, dowsing rods or whatever, but a good deal harder to work out what the reactions might mean.

It is also worth looking at the work first described by Michel-Eugene Chevreul, who was born in Paris in 1876 and is more famous for making candles and for work on the psychology of colour. He attached a pendulum to the end of a 20-40-centimetre-long rod and held it over a cross drawn on a sheet of paper. The idea was to hold the device like a fishing rod with the pendulum over the middle of the cross. He would start the weight swinging in any direction or just leave it hanging on its own accord. At the same time, Chevreul would concentrate on one of the four directions of the cross. The pendulum, very quickly, would take up that exact direction. With a bit of practice, one can make it swing in any direction using nothing other than brainpower. So, dowsers can cheat to their heart's content, and sadly, a good number of pseudo dowsers cheat themselves without even knowing it.

Even something as simple as meditating is fraught with pitfalls; someone trying this for the first time will not know whether they are just resting or entering a state of deep meditation. Therefore it is much easier to have help from someone who has done it before. Some helpers will try to accelerate the process by using drugs or suggesting smoking dried plants. Both can be expensive and prove fatal. There are no short cuts. It can take a while to learn techniques and it could take even longer to perfect them, but there is no way in which drugs are going to improve the process. They are only going to make matters worse. Virtually everything that can be achieved with drugs can also be done without them, and the advantage of doing without is that the person keeps himself in control of his own body and can 'kick out' of any condition almost instantly, when he wants to. Drugs no not have any place within a Traditional Witchcraft coven.

Reaching a state of deep meditation can be speeded up with a hypnotic induction, so it worth learning how this is done. When entering such a state the nervous system becomes far more sensitive and the subject is more likely to hear, smell or even 'see' things with his eyes closed. This means he is likely to react faster to emergencies than when not in such a trance-like state. However, there is a difference between being in such a condition and sleeping. There is no point in relaxing deeply if all the body needs is some well-deserved sleep. Showmen diviners use crystal balls to make themselves look impressive, so that their customers think the money spent at an amusement arcade was worth it. Genuine diviners use mirrors, crystal balls or similar aids to shut down their optic nerve so that their senses become sharper and they are more responsive to energy around them. Do bear in mind that so-called psychics do not have special powers installed in them by an outside power and they are not born with any extraordinary ability – they learned the trade. Anyone and everyone can carry out such psychic methods. The problem is that not everybody learning to play the piano will become a concert pianist and not everyone can become a brilliant medium, but everybody can benefit from such techniques for their own ends.

It is important to remember that it is best to work with a good mentor; and help from like-minded friends will make the learning process much easier than going it alone.

Unexpected Effects of Joining a Coven or Dabbling with Natural Energy

Some things like cycling, swimming and conjuring tricks need to be learned once for us to master them for the rest of our lives, but magic, dowsing, meditation and working with natural energy does not produce results all the time. There is some evidence that some aspects might be tide dependent, even when one is a long way from the sea, and they could also be influenced by biorhythms or other outside influences.

Reasons why divination does not work all the time:
You are too tense.
There is too much on your mind.
There are too many distractions.
You are tired.
You are dowsing for the wrong reason.
You are asking for something you want rather than something you need.
You are in the wrong environment.
You are surrounded by the wrong people.
You are surrounded by antagonism.
You are surrounded by too many sceptics.
You are doing it to show off.
You have no interest in the subject.
You cannot visualise what you are trying to dowse.
It is not the right time. Try again later.
You are under pressure to produce results.
You are not asking the right question.
There are too many distractions.
You are wearing a watch with battery or a magnetic bracelet.

Once one has enjoyed the passwords of 'perfect love and perfect trust' in a safe coven, one is likely to be confronted with other major happenings as a result of dropping into deeply relaxed states. Psychologists and clinical hypnotherapists have identified different levels of deep relaxed states. This does not mean that one is likely to drop from one into another, like falling down a staircase, but one could be confronted by slightly different feelings at different times and the sequence and effects of these could be most variable. It is virtually impossible to predict feelings and one is unlikely to notice anything happening while going into a semi-conscious state. If one does notice then the conscious mind will have been engaged and the process is likely to stop.

The following are some natural results from meditation or going into a deeply relaxed state. These could happen to anyone at any time when entering a state of deep relaxation and they are not always the result of any supernatural occurrences.

1. Physical relaxation leading to mental relaxation and perhaps drowsiness can make the body feel light or heavy. It could be that the person is so tired that he will immediately drop off to sleep.
2. Eyelids become rigid and opening the eyes requires considerable effort.
3. Limbs feel rigid and moving them becomes difficult.
4. The breathing rate slows down.
5. Heartbeat slows down.
6. Sexual arousal. Sadly society has made this a prohibited zone and sexual arousal can make the conscious mind take control, preventing the subject from slipping further into a relaxed state. On the other hand, if the subject is with another person and they choose to have intercourse, then they are hopelessly diverted from the main aim of finding the state of semi-consciousness.
7. Elated feelings of lightness, as if one has been on a long restful holiday for a long time. This can make one feel as if they are floating in air. People who have had contact with the Alexander Technique of Relaxation will know about the *Whispered Ah*, which can be a great help because it can release more energy from the body.
8. The skin and especially the face become very sensitive. There is a fizzy sensation on the skin and it feels as if it is made of china, which is about to crack.
9. The rest of the body becomes very sensitive.
10. Hearing improves and one becomes aware of sounds that cannot normally be heard. This is absolutely weird and almost impossible to describe in words. On the one hand you cannot hear noisy distractions around you, but on the other hand you can hear other sounds that are normally not heard.
11. A feeling of detachment from the body.

12. Temporary loss of memory. This happens to many people and almost everybody must have been travelling along a familiar route without the slightest knowledge of having passed through a long chain of obstacles.

13. An illusion of smell or being touched or seeing things that aren't there. These three do not normally come together and one is likely to experience only one at a time. Don't think of this being a mild case of the imagination playing tricks. The stimulation can be so powerful with strong emotions that the subject has no way of knowing whether the experience was real or not.

14. Temporary loss of sensations. This is difficult to comprehend and to explain, especially as the senses normally improve when the body and mind are deeply relaxed. It is possible to find oneself in a most uncomfortable position without feeling the discomfort.

15. Total body rigidity making it impossible to move, but this tends to stop as soon as the conscious mind takes control. However, if the body has been in such a state for a long time, it might take a while for the blood circulation to catch up and one might experience 'pins and needles' before full body control is established.

16. Time hallucination or illusion. When relaxed time seems to pass much slower. When asked to guess for how long they have been in a state of semi-consciousness, the majority of people will guess a quarter or a third of the real time. This time discrepancy is most variable and experienced relaxers can make the time ten, twenty or thirty times longer or shorter than the length of the actual experience.

This chapter can provide nothing more than a brief oversight, to hopefully explain that these are not subjects for lone experimentation and an experienced helper will be more than useful. By going it alone one is more likely to drop oneself into uncomfortable situations and it will be difficult to know how much has been achieved. Do remember that you do not have to climb to the top of the mountain, but it is a great help if you know where the summits might be. There are far too many people with elementary abilities pretending to be experts. However, a Traditional Witchcraft coven can guide and help people through problems that might arise.

ILLUSTRATED GLOSSARY

Alchemy Alchemy has often been belittled by saying it was mainly concerned with ridiculous activities such as trying to make valuable substances like gold and silver from base metals. However, the alchemists of the past were in fact the extraordinary forerunners of our modern chemists. There is evidence to suggest that mankind has been dabbling with all kinds of materials since time immemorial and there are plenty of indications that early man made fantastic strides with his understanding of substances or chemicals as they are now known. Sadly such exploratory work was looked upon as being against the teachings of the Church and much of it was prohibited for several centuries.

Alexandrian covens Witchcraft covens that started springing up during the mid 1950s as a result of infiltration of followers of Alex Sanders.

Altar A small flat topped block, table or cloth laid on a flat surface for the purpose of religious focus.

Amulet An object or charm said to have magical properties.

Analytical psychology Examining and/or treating mental conditions such as phobias or undesirable habits by bringing to light repressions in a person's unconscious mind that could be influencing behaviour and/or reactions. This can be done with hypnosis. Information on how this is done can be obtained from the International Association of Hypnotherapists.

Angels Natural forces or spiritual beings usually with good intentions, often humanised and given Christian names.

Astral Plane The state or dimension into which the souls pass immediately following physical death. It lies between the physical and the mental planes. It is a plane of instincts, emotions and fluidity. This is the plane whereby occultists do their work and the witches bring their spells to fruition.

Astral Projection *See* Out of Body Experience.

Athame A black handled knife used by Traditional Witchcraft covens for ceremonial purposes and therefore without sharp edges so that it cannot inflict accidental injuries. It is said to have male characteristics and is a personal tool of the witch.

Archetypes Ancient mental images which are present in the collective unconscious and which can determine thinking and behavioural patterns. They may be accessed through symbols and/or rituals.

Athames for sale in the
Cauldron of Inspiration in
Folkestone (Kent).

Aura An energy field surrounding plants, animals, humans and some inanimate
objects such as rocks; often depicted in old paintings as a halo around
the head. This subject requires further serious study with down-to-earth
experimentation and is most fascinating to look into. The big problem is that
a great deal of nonsense has been written about it as well and it is difficult
for any casual dabbler to distinguish between facts and fiction. Therefore the
best results are achieved through further exploration with serious thought
and good experimentation, rather than reading books. The strength of the
aura is influenced by diet, smoking, consuming excessive alcohol, lack of
rest, not being fit and other factors.

Beltane An ancient Celtic fire festival celebrated on May eve through to May
Day, marking the beginning of the old Celtic summer. Bel was a Celtic Sun
God and Taine means fire.

Besom See broom.

Blessed Be Greeting used by Traditional witches. Also known as the five-fold kiss.
It is the witch's way of greeting or parting from another witch. Blessed be implies
the entire five-fold kiss in the ritual circle and happens particularly at initiations.

Blood Traditional Witchcraft is not concerned with bloody activities. The
drawing of blood or inflicting injuries is not part of the Old Religion,
although such obscene methods are used by some covens.

Boline A knife, usually with a white handle, used for practical purposes such as cutting plants, fruit or food.

Book of Shadows Known in Traditional covens merely as *The Book*. A personal notebook, either as book for writing in by hand or as loose-leaf folder for holding typed information of what has been learnt and should not be forgotten, especially the order of rituals and the uses of natural resources.

Brocken The highest point of the German Harz Mountains where witches were reputed to meet for special sabbats, but no one seems to have witnessed any of these events. At 1,141 metres (3742 feet) it is the highest point in northern Europe with a unique microclimate resembling higher Alpine altitudes. It is also the last part of high ground of the North European Plain before reaching the Ural Mountains in Russia. The top is often shrouded in mists and its granite outcrops resemble the tors of Dartmoor, giving the summit a mystical appearance. These days there is a railway running to a radio station, with a huge aerial mast, on the top. (For comparison: Snowdon in Wales is 1,085 m and Ben Nevis 1,344 m high.)

Broomsticks Possibly the first weapon a woman might reach for when surprised by hostile visitors. Considerable volumes of rubbish has been written about brooms and in east European folklore they could be replaced by any long handled gardening or farming implement, such as rakes, hoes or shepherd crooks and used for a variety of so-called satanic activities like flying through the air. Nowadays they are used to ritually sweep a room before the circle is opened.

Celts Celts did not originate in Scotland, Wales, Cornwall or Ireland, but were driven there by advancing Roman authoritarianism. At one time, before the Romans introduced Latin, the Celtic languages with several different dialects

189

A Roman and Celtic re-enactment group on Folkestone's East Cliff. Such groups are often an excellent source of information.

were widespread across Europe; early Bronze Age people living near the Black Sea would probably have understood people living as far away as Portugal, France, Germany and Britain. Yet, despite this common language and its associated culture being spread so widely over Europe, there never was a united Celtic empire. The Romans drove the Celts into Europe's extremities, where remnants of the early culture remained. Although a number of the Celtic languages died out relatively recently, patches of several dialects remained and are now being rekindled by the media and governments, so that areas such as Wales have become bilingual again. Interestingly enough, the early Celts have left Britain with far richer archaeology than some of the more dominant later cultures of England.

Chalice The elemental tool of the water element, which is feminine in nature.

Channelling Other than the obvious dictionary definitions, channelling has a number of meanings, all of them somewhat vague. So it is necessary to ask anyone using this word what they actually mean. The common meaning is to direct energy along a particular route or to absorb energy or information from one person to another. This seems to work very well when the conditions are right. There are also other, more specific New Age meanings.

Circle Wiccan rituals are carried out inside a circle. This is usually an imaginary line and is not marked by any visible means. It can be any size, depending on the space available or the number of people needing to be accommodated.

Clairvoyance There are a number of slightly varying definitions for this word and many people associate it entirely with fortune telling, which is not correct. 'The power of sensing actions or objects beyond the natural range of the normal senses' would perhaps make the best definition, but it is important to remember that any practitioners are entertainers and therefore nothing more than stage conjurers. Yet, there are others who are extremely accurate and come up with such amazing information that there is no way that trickery can be involved. The important point to bear in mind is that, like dowsing, this is something that can be learned and therefore the vast majority of people can become clairvoyants in some way. Not everybody will necessarily be terribly good at it, but everybody can use it to their own personal advantage. The important first question to ask any clairvoyant is not what is going to happen tomorrow, but without giving any indications, ask what happened in the past. When doing this there are people who will relate the most amazing incidents, almost as if they were there when they happened. True clairvoyants are difficult to identify because they look just like every other ordinary person and one will only get to know about their abilities when they start talking. Any clairvoyant turning up in fancy dress or accompanied by a vast array of accoutrements is best avoided. Some of them are truly amazing, both in ability and fancy appearance.

Collective Unconscious The name for a shared pool of memories and knowledge, which people and animals can tap into. This idea from the science of analytical psychology was proposed by Dr Carl Jung and goes some way towards explaining how 'inherited memories' might function.

Cone of Power Visualised as a cone shape rising from the centre of the ritual circle. It is an energy field composed from the energies of practitioners creating it. These can also be seen naturally in rivers or in other moving liquids. *See also* vortex.

Corn Dolly Although some books about old country crafts would want us to believe that there were special trades people specialising in the making of corn dollies, it would seem that this was an amateur skill practiced by everybody who grew cereal crops. Many cultures have habits of looking after the souls of the animals they hunt and the crops they harvest. Corn dollies probably started out as mere bunch of dried cereals kept in a warm, dry place throughout the winter so that the corn spirit could live in comfort until it was released the following year, hopefully to encourage a plentiful harvest. At one time one could see a vast variety of corn dollies and even after the Second World War they still formed a significant part of agricultural shows. Sadly, now the art seems to be dying, possibly because plants with shorter and shorter stems are now producing cereal crops. In the 1950s it was still common to find large fields so high that a nine to ten-year-old child could not look over the top without standing on some higher vantage point. Now the seed heads are much lower, making it more difficult to make dollies from them.

Country Crafts Trades, crafts and skills carried out in country districts and usually handed down from master to apprentice.

Coven A coven is a Witchcraft or Wiccan group that may be governed by a

group of Elders and led by a High Priest and High Priestess. Females wishing to join such a group must ask the High Priest and males the High Priestess. The applicant is then brought before the Elders, who decide whether that person should be initiated or not. This is explained in Chapter 2.

Covenstead The coven's meeting place.

Craft The Craft is an alternative word for Witchcraft, Wicca and the Old Religion.

Crystals A crystal is an orderly arrangement of tiny particles or 'building blocks' that produce natural distinct shapes, often with flat surfaces and well-defined edges. Some substances are capable of producing a series of different shapes, while others always develop identical crystals. Some substances crystallise easily, while others hardly ever develop these distinctive shapes. To make matters more confusing, some substances sometimes produce crystal shapes usually associated with another mineral. The crystals themselves can be microscopically small or so huge that they are much bigger than a person. Small crystal varieties can form huge irregular lumps and some rocks are made up of a variety of different crystals. Granite, for example, is usually made up of quartz, feldspar and mica. Pure, good quality crystals can command exceedingly high prices, especially when they are made of a rare mineral. Crystals have been attributed magical powers and are used for specific purposes and healing techniques. This has developed in recent years and there are now a good number of books describing the properties of crystals, but most of them do not explain the experimentation that was used to discover their secrets.

Tumble polished pebbles are often sold as crystals, so it is necessary to be aware that a crystal has a natural shape, which it created on its own without man's interference. Some of these are damaged when mined, quarried or dug out of the ground and some specimens then have their faces polished by hand. This retains the original crystal shape, but with a false, man-made surface. Tumble polished stones can, of course, be made up of a crystallising mineral, with the crystals themselves so small that they cannot be seen without a magnifying glass.

Some people, especially those needing to draw attention to themselves,

Fluorite.

Selenite.

Calcite.   Marcasite.

claim they can feel the energy emitted from crystals as a stabbing pain. Yet, it would appear that this can only be felt when they can also see the crystal and they cannot feel the pain when someone holds such powerful crystals by their back without them being aware of the mineral's presence. So, there is ample of room for experimentation in this field.

Cycles It would seem likely that early man lived exceedingly close to nature, following the yearly or natural cycles in order to survive and this became even more important when it came to planting crops at the right time of the year. Bearing in mind that preparatory work often had to be done long before there were marked changes in seasonal weather, he must have had a good knowledge of what we now call the yearly calendar.

Adhering to the natural cycles became less important once people started living in towns and cities, where they had to adapt to neighbours and services provided by other people, rather than rely on nature. This stark difference in lifestyles meant it was possible for a proportion of people to arrange their time in any way they liked and it allowed them to pursue unnatural activities. Thus they could adapt their daily lives to fit in with what was dictated by authorities. The Church may also have dominated people living in the countryside, but there it was also necessary to keep the natural cycles in sight and activities had to be arranged to fit in with what nature demanded. The long summer school holidays are a relic of bygone times when all spare hands, including those of children, were required to help with harvesting. The autumn half term holidays were called 'potato holidays' across vast areas of northern Europe because children were required in the fields to help bring the valuable harvest to the farms. Thus a sort of two tier system of living developed throughout northern Europe and this lasted until well after the Second World War when a new car-dominated and car-worshipping society made it possible to reach the deepest rural areas and transform those districts beyond all recognition. As a result the natural cycles died out while the countryside was turned into dormitories for the towns and crops are grown by contractors (rather than farmers) by adding vast volumes of artificial chemicals.

Dagger *See* athame.

Degrees of Study Traditional Witchcraft covens, operational before Gerald Gardner published his book *Witchcraft Today*, initiate members into five degrees: earth, water, air, fire and spirit, but the new Gardnerian and Alexandrian covens initiate to only three degrees. See Chapter 6.

Devil A supreme power of evil and the keeper of Hell (also called Satan). This is a Christian concept and it not recognised by those of the Old Religion. It seems strange that many awe-inspiring natural wonders are named after the devil and hardly any have been named after saints. For example there is the Devil's Dyke, Punchbowl, Causeway, Bridge, Leap, Walk, Bellows, Frying Pan, Hole, Stack, Kneading Trough and probably many more.

Divination Determining the location of hidden objects, information or energies, or finding out what the future has in store, but not fortune telling. This played a considerable part in many ancient civilisations and is still practised with great enthusiasm by large numbers of people using a vast variety of different methods. Whilst the subject is dominated by conjurers and used for entertainment, there are many other aspects, which can be proven to work exceedingly well, although no one has ever explained satisfactorily exactly how the methods work. Anyone wanting to study this field in depth is advised to contact the British Society of Dowsers, which provides some fascinating training courses where results can be verified.

Divine Power Pure, natural energy, the life force of all things on earth and what many religions call 'God'.

Dowsing Searching for hidden objects, energies, water or whatever, by using a wide variety of tools. This is something everybody can learn and a good way to start is to contact the British Society of Dowsers, who conduct a number of training courses and provide help for accomplished dowsers.

Druid Celtic priests, prophets, soothsayers and magicians from the pre-Christian era, about which very little is known. They held oak trees to be sacred, reputedly built Stonehenge and cut mistletoe with golden sickles. However, Stonehenge is known to be a few thousand years older than the first Druids and cutting anything with soft gold implements is not the easiest of tasks. The Druids formed an important core in the early Iron Age and provided the Romans with some food for thought, especially as far as their knowledge of mathematics, astronomy and therefore natural cycles was concerned.

Earth Mother Natural energy that exists to give life to plants and animals, to provide fertility and thus create a good harvest. The Earth Mother, as the female aspect of deity, is the personification of these forces of nature.

Egregore An astral light body formed by practitioners and animated by divine plane emotions. It is a way that the practitioner can establish a communication with the divine.

Elders Originally the governing body of a Traditional Witchcraft coven, which helps to select and appoint new members for initiation. Only the High Priest and High Priestess know the identity of the elders.

Elements, Aristotelian This refers to five elements recognised by Traditional Witchcraft covens – earth, water, air, fire and spirit – and should not be confused with the elements of the periodic table.

Elementals Natural entities that are of the essence of one of the four elements and are from another order of creation. They can also be created by humans as a thought form and then gain a semi-independent existence. This type is often used for healing and protection, but can also be used in physic attacks.

Endless Knot A pentagram or five-sided star is called an endless knot because it can be drawn without lifting pen from paper.

Energy fields Around a body, *see* aura.

Eostre Teutonic goddess of spring after whom Easter is named.

Equinox The times of the year when the sun is passing directly over the equator, making the hours of darkness the same as the hours of daylight. This happens on 21 March (spring equinox in northern latitudes) and 22 September (autumn equinox in northern latitudes).

Ergot Influence Ergot is a fungus with the scientific name of *Claviceps purpurea*, which grows in seed heads of grasses and cereal crops and was known since at least the Middle Ages, but not fully understood until it was analysed during the twentieth century. It is deadly poisonous if eaten in large enough quantities. It seems likely that it was responsible for killing off almost everybody in the same village at the same time. The Christian Church labelled it as punishment for the sinners. Despite it probably having been recognised as poisonous, it was used as a medicine and as an aid to help childbirth. When eaten in small enough quantities, not strong enough to kill, it could result in creating convulsions, hallucinations and other forms of strange behaviour. It seems likely that the poorer, perhaps older people, especially older widows, were condemned to eating it because they could not afford the better quality grain, thus making people think that their weird ailment was due to them being in league with the devil. It is still used to today for the manufacture of several modern medicines including a relief for migraines.

Esbat A coven meeting that is not one of the sabbats. It is often held on a full moon period but in Traditional Witchcraft it is often used as a teaching session.

Fairies' Tree A powerful energy centre. The dryad or fairy elemental is the tree's guardian spirit, protecting it from harm.

Fertility Fertility refers to an organism's ability to reproduce, rather than the number of offspring they can provide. This subject is still shrouded in considerable mystery, bigotry and weird contradictions. Until relatively recently it was assumed that only men or males can reproduce by planting their 'seeds' inside a female; this gave rise to succession always following the male line. Early man must have known that females were far more receptive for creating offspring at certain periods and the understanding of these natural cycles was essential for survival. It is also strange that this has become such a taboo subject, even in modern society, despite mankind having studied it in the greatest detail ever since the beginning of time.

Fetish Fetish can refer to any objects worshipped by people and it is in this connection that it is used in this book, but it also could mean anything that is looked upon by one person as being something abnormal and used for some unconnected purpose. For example some people can mange to obtain sexual satisfaction from objects like worn socks or smelly shoes. In such cases the object replaces another human as a basic object to love.

Fire Wheel A solar symbol. The flaming wheel can be rolled downhill, especially in summertime to signify the start of the sun's weakening powers.

Five Elements (Aristotelian) Traditional Witchcraft covens initiate members through five degrees: earth, water, air, fire and spirit.

Gardnerian covens Wicca covens that started springing up during the mid 1950s after the publication of the book *Witchcraft Today* by Gerald Gardner.

Great Rite The bringing together of the male and female principles through sacred, ritual, sexual intercourse.

Greater Sabbats The four great yearly pre-Christian fire festivals celebrated by Druids and the Celts. The festivals are: Imbolg (Candlemas) on 1 February, Beltane on May Eve, Lugnasadh (Lammas) on August Eve and Samhain (Halloween) on November Eve.

Handfasting Joining two people who love each other, as in marriage or blessing their marriage if they married outside Wiccan circles.

Hand Maiden The Handmaiden assists the High Priestess during rituals. The Maiden may or may not be the High Priestess' understudy.

Hedge Witch *See* Witch, Hedge

Herbalism A herb tends to be a plant without woody stems that dies down for the winter and which can be used for medicinal purposes. However, herbalism also includes the collection, preparation, storage and use of all substances derived from plants and used for food, medicines, flavouring, colouring or whatever. It is important to learn this from experienced practitioners, even if only going on occasional courses or taking part in sporadic fieldwork. The main reason is that many useful plants, especially fungi, have poisonous counterparts, which can look almost identical to the useful one. Studying this subject is very much a personal matter and people are advised to concentrate on those plants they can find easily, although going out to hunt for rare specimens can be most exciting. Local natural history groups often provide good introductions.

High Priest The most senior male priest and leader of a Witchcraft coven.

High Priestess The most senior female priestess and overall leader of a Witchcraft coven.

Horned God The masculine, virile and earthy side of nature is personified as the Horned God (of the witches) and often thought of as the god *Cernunnos*. The Horned God of the old religions was turned into the devil by the Christian Church and is often represented as an evil figure.

Hypnotherapy Using hypnosis for examining and/or treating mental conditions such as phobias or undesirable habits by bringing to light repressions in a person's unconscious mind that could be influencing behaviour and/or reactions. Works also without hypnosis, but then takes much longer and then tends be called Psychoanalysis. Anyone wanting to study this might consider contacting the International Association of Hypnotherapists.

Illusions Something a person perceives to be real but doesn't exist or something, which gives a wrong impression. Optical illusions are probably the most well known, although it is possible to produce illusions with other senses as well. Illusions are used commonly in advertising and marketing where people are often given false information but believe it to be true or they are misled by the advert.

Imbolg A festival celebrated on 1 February to mark the beginning of spring. Imbolg or Oimelc, a Celtic word for Ewes Milk, and was the early spring Celtic fire festival. Nowadays it is the start of the lambing season and signifies the increasing light as well as the appearance of the first green shoots. This festival is also sacred to the old Celtic goddess Brigid.

Inherited memory Some memory or instinct or natural knowledge, call it what you like, appears to be inherited or drawn from the collective unconscious. No one has ever explained how this works but there is ample evidence that people come by information without having learnt it the usual way. Perhaps one of the best illustrations for this is the cuckoo. Cuckoos never meet their parents so there is no way that they can be taught how to behave as a cuckoo, yet they all manage to live most complicated life cycles and seem to know exactly how to behave.

Inquisition A deep and thorough investigation but also used to describe the witch hunts of the Middle Ages when the Christians persecuted, tortured and put to death everyone opposing their doctrine.

Irrlicht See Will-o'-the-Wisp.

Kabbalah alternate spelling for Qabalah.

Keeper The most senior member of a Traditional Witchcraft coven's Elders. The Elders usually wear white robes and the Keeper can be distinguished from the rest by his/her brown robe.

Kim's Game A game used for visualisation training where people are allowed to look at about twenty-five or so objects for a minute and then have about four minutes to write down as many objects as they remember through visualisation without seeing them while writing.

Kiss, Five-fold The ritual kissing on both feet, both knees, the vulva or penis, both breasts and the lips. This is only used in the coven circle and is given man-to-woman or woman-to-man.

Kundalini This is another one of those strange terms that has been botched by so many ill-informed people that one is left with a heap of complicated garbage that is most difficult to understand. It would seem that Kundalini is a form of energy that lies dormant in the base chakra and can be made

Whether the coven works sky clad or wears gowns, initiation is always in the nude because it is like a rebirth. It is the body or the person that starts a new life without any accoutrements attached to it. Newcomers are greeted with the five-fold kiss – females by the High Priest and males by the High Priestess.

to rise, producing a burst of unexpected energy, perhaps similar to coming to an orgasm but without any sexual activity. One person described it as a type of liquid fire bursting through the body, which Bill agreed with. When Kundalini pierces the final chakra, illumination and enlightenment can occur. Another member of Bill's coven who tried raising Kundalini on his own, having been given some guidance from Bill, was so overwhelmed and surprised that he abandoned his attempt. This is, of course, the great advantage of using help from a coven rather than drugs because it is easier to pull out of any strange situation by engaging the conscious mind and thus cancelling the process. Having a knowledgeable person to help with this process can be most useful. I have experienced this once or twice and if that is true, then there is no way that the burst of liquid fire came from within me. It felt far more like sitting or lying on an energy point and feeling something burst out of ground below. Other people who have experienced it say that it feels as if it starts from without, but it is actually from within.

Lesser Sabbats These are the equinoxes and solstices. At the spring and autumn equinoxes the sun crosses the Equator, giving equal day and night hours. The position of the sun, overhead at the Tropic of Cancer, gives the northern hemisphere the Summer Solstice or the longest day. When the sun is overhead at the Tropic of Capricorn it gives us the Winter Solstice or the shortest day.

Lughnasadh A festival celebrated on 1 August, marking the beginning of the first harvest in northern Europe. One of the greater sabbats celebrated by ancient Celts as a great fire festival, signifying the first harvest on August Eve. Lugh was a Celtic god of light.

Magic To change things or to boost things by channelling natural energy.

Magic, Black Another term for evil magic.

Maypole A decorated pole for dancing around on Mayday. Many towns and villages in Catholic-dominated southern Germany have massive maypoles in their centres, often painted in the Bavarian colours of white and light blue. They also feature in many country districts throughout northern Europe. A phallic symbol.

Mead An alcoholic drink made with fermented honey. Widespread in northern Europe in the olden days when it formed a major drink together with beer, cider and fermented fruit juices. Mead is often drunk after a sabbat.

Mighty Ones Spirit forces or natural energy, often humanised and given names.

Moon Goddess The goddess aspect in the sky comprising of the waxing, full and waning of the moon. These, in turn, are symbolised by the maid, the mother and the crone.

Moon, Drawing Down Invoking of the Goddess energy into the high priestess by the high priest.

Mother, Great She is the female personification of the forces and powers of all nature. New life is constantly generated by the limitless fertility of the great mother along with the virility of her consort, the God.

New Age Ideas and thoughts put forward as an alternative to the established culture, religion, medicine etc. It would seem that people are constantly inventing or discovering new secrets and putting these forward to replace what has been going on before. Though, others have described many of these 'new' discoveries long ago.

Occult Originally occult meant the study of the unknown, secret or mysterious, but today it strongly suggests some connection with mystical or supernatural happenings. It is a philosophy that explores the meaning of life in a rational way while moving beyond both physical science and psychology. The exact meaning of the word varies with who is using it; the majority who toss it about do not fully understand exactly what the unknown, secret or mysterious is.

Old Religion Another word for Witchcraft, Wicca or the Craft.

Organic Gardening and Organic Foods There is no reason at all why Wiccans should suddenly change to using organic produce if they cannot afford the higher prices that need to be paid for such foods. However, many do so because consistency, flavour and benefit from such foods tend to be superior to those produced with artificial chemicals. Organic gardening is concerned with using and recycling materials for best advantage and planting species that get on well together. Organic gardeners usually do not dig the soil, but add self-made compost instead. This prevents earthworms from being killed and forms a natural soil. The Henry Doubleday Research Association has a number of organic gardens open to the public and also publishes a list when private gardens are open for inspection.

Out of body experience A sense of parting from the body following a near death experience. Also known as astral projection and remote viewing.

Pagan This is another one of those words that has been hijacked by the media and had its meaning twisted beyond recognition. Originally Pagans were people living in rural areas who acknowledged the existence of some spirit force. Modern Pagans are happy to worship natural forces and they refer to them in a variety of terms. At the same time they try to live in harmony with nature and to learn how this can best be done. They do not follow any of the more modern religions with their own saints or gods but prefer to follow what nature has to offer.

Pentacle 1. A circle with a pentagram inside it or engraved on it. Used ritually to represent the earth element. 2. A five-pointed star within the circle is used as a magical or mystical symbol by Pagans. It represents both the human being and the four elements of earth, water, fire and air, governed by spirit.

Pentagram A five-sided star.

Philosopher's Stone A substance that can prolong life, heal wounds and illnesses and change base metals into gold and silver. It has never been identified and almost certainly does not exist.

Power Cone *See* Cone of Power

Qabalah Alternative spelling for Kabbalah or Cabbala.

Remote Viewing *See* Out of Body Experience.

Repressed Memories People who have not gone through a full hypnoanalysis will have a good number of repressed memories that are so well hidden in their subconscious that they has no knowledge whatsoever that the information is in their mind. These repressions can produce phobias, undesirable behaviour or other mental problems. Anyone wanting to study this further is advised to consult the International Association of Hypnotherapists.

Rituals One of the great aims of many religions that do not have massive prayer books is to talk to the unconscious mind and this should be done without using words or normal language. The process of shutting down normal senses and usual channels of communication can take a while, and can be so difficult that the majority will not reach such a state of mind. Remembering the sequence of how to reach such a deep state of mind by using words and reading from prayer books is self-defeating as the conscious mind prevents anyone from entering states of really deep meditation. So, Wiccan covens have developed a series of rituals to guide them along the right route. There are a wide variety of ways in which states of deep meditation can be achieved and they can all work. The big problem is to get there without engaging the conscious mind; rituals with chanting and music help a great deal in remembering sequences.

Rock worship *See* stones

Runes The old Nordic alphabet, probably adapted from the Latin around the second century AD and used throughout northern Europe as far south as the Mediterranean, although far more common in more northern latitudes. The letters inscribed on wood, stone, bone and any other materials early were also attributed magical properties and used for divination. A number of different systems were developed in different areas and at different times and much of this system of communication seems to have died out as a result of the Inquisition, which associated runes with black magic and Witchcraft. Despite this, the writing of runes remained a communication system throughout northern Europe and were, more recently, resurrected by the National Socialists in Germany. As a result they were banned in Germany at the end of the Second World War. It would seem that many people in Germany are deeply frightened by these simple symbols. Still today, German model makers who displayed them on their work found themselves hounded

by the police when these were displayed at exhibitions. The swastika was a symbol for the Earth Mother and Hitler's Schutzstaffel or SS (Guards Division) used Runes rather than Latin letters on their badges.

Sabbat The eight seasonal festivals celebrated by witches.

Sabbath The seventh day of the week, a day for rest; Saturdays for Jews and Sundays for Christians.

Samhain One of the eight seasonal festivals. Samhain marks the old Celtic new year and the onset of winter. It is a time to honour the ancestors and dead friends.

Satan Another name for Devil.

Scourge A whip used by Traditional Witchcraft covens for symbolic ritual purification, but not for beating people or objects.

Sky-clad A witch's ritual nakedness.

Sky Father The god whose aspect in the sky is usually as a sun god figure. He has a horned god aspect, which can be related to the waxing and the waning years as well as to virility.

Solstice The times of year when the sun is furthest away from the equator. In the northern hemisphere the Summer Solstice is on about 21 June, when the sun is over the Tropic of Cancer and in winter on about 22 December, when the sun is over the Tropic of Capricorn. Witches celebrate these times as two of the lesser sabbats.

Speak to unconscious or subconscious mind For the purpose of this book unconscious mind and subconscious mind are both taken to refer to that part of brain which cannot be accessed with normal thought. The unconscious mind cannot calculate nor reason and it is quite likely that it won't understand words either. For that reason Traditional Witchcraft covens do not read from prayer books when meditating. Instead they use the simplest of words so that every person can visualise what they want to understand. This is terribly important and a fundamental requirement of deep meditation techniques. In a way, one can equate meditation with prayer, but words are not used. When 'speaking to the unconscious mind' it is necessary to use as many senses as possible to get the right 'feeling' for what one is trying to express. An example mentioned elsewhere in this book is that anyone thinking of water could easily confuse the subconscious by forming images of a tap, a bucket, a hosepipe, a river, a lake or so on. Speaking to the unconscious mind is not easy, but it can be very effective when done properly. This is used by a vast variety of religions, all in slightly different ways, but all producing similar results.

Spells The art of causing change through a magical ritual.

Spiral *See* Vortex.

Springs *See* Water.

Stone Circles and Standing Stones There are a vast number of standing stones throughout northern Europe and similar structures further south. Many of these were erected during the late Stone Age when mankind already had some knowledge of how to work bronze, but there are others that are even earlier and seem to have been erected during the early Stone Age. Bearing in mind that some of the stones for building Stonehenge were brought from Pembrokeshire, some 180 miles (290 km) away, it would seem that early man had a highly organised society and could not only describe how to find his way over such vast distances, but also make the arrangements for many people to turn up at the same time at the same place and provide workers with food. In a way, this organisation seems to be far more difficult to solve than the problem of moving and raising the huge stones. Some stone circles are relatively small, but others, such as the site at Carnac in northern France, consist of over 3,000 huge menhirs. The fact that early man chose to use such huge boulders might suggest that their exact location was important and that they shouldn't be shifted into slightly different positions. Could it also suggest that the stone circles were left unattended for long periods each year when unscrupulous people might have changed the formation?

Stones The ice ages left exceedingly large numbers of boulders scattered erratically over much of northern Europe; many of these were removed from arable fields to make ploughing easier. Most of them were round and not much use for building unless cement was also available, so for a long time and over a large area they were looked upon as nuisances rather than assets. Some were moved to act as boundary markers or placed along the sides of tracks, and bigger ones were transported considerable distances to mark graves or were used for indicating spots where meetings took place.

One exception is the Blue Stone in Russia, which still today attracts

a considerable number of travellers and even supports a small souvenir industry, although it is hardly signposted and quite difficult to find if one doesn't know its exact location. The Blue Stone, consisting of roughly 12-tons of basalt, had healing powers attributed to it long before Christians ventured into the area around Lake Pleshcheyevo near the town of Pereslavl-Zalessy, to the north-east of Moscow, in what is now a magnificent national park. A famous stone with healing properties had to have some connection with the devil and the first Christians moved it away from its resting place. Apparently they dropped it into the water of the lake or buried it, or possibly both at different times. The annoying point was that all efforts to get rid of the heavy object were to no avail and it reappeared in its designated resting place all on its own. The place was (and still is) remote enough for the local Christians not to have noticed little groups of Pagans aiding the process, although such blasphemous activity could well have cost the perpetrators their lives. After all, the first Christians in those far-off wild areas obtained a high conversion rate to Christianity because they killed those who didn't want to join the new club. So, on the surface many locals supported the new regime as long as authority was keeping a watchful eye, but they quickly reverted to their old ways once they were alone. Yet, it wasn't necessary to travel terribly far away from main centres to be well out of the way of general scrutiny and among the isolation of the harsh country, it was essential to live in harmony with nature or perish.

The Inquisition to rid society of witches didn't seem to have stretched far into Russia at all and even today devout Christians are happy to admit that their best monasteries were built on recognised Pagan sites. What is even

A number of rocks were placed on top of packet of photographic papers and left for several days. Some of them were radioactive and contaminated the photographic plate as can be seen here. This shows that energy radiating out of these stones passed through several layers of paper.

more astonishing for anyone from the West is that these Christians are quite happy to go to church, participate in yoga and then do some dowsing.

The question of whether stones contain or are capable of generating energy can be answered by a simple experiment. One the easiest ways of doing this is to rub two pieces of flat quartz in a dark location and one will see that they illuminate, almost as if there is a light bulb inside them. It is also possible to place some granite from Cornwall onto photographic paper, leave it in position for several weeks and then develop the paper in the normal way. This will show that particles from the stones travelled through several layers of paper and clouded it the same way, as light would have done, although light was never allowed to come into contact with the paper.

It is possible that the glowing quartz gave rise to the Rhine Gold Legend, where we are told that dwarves live on the bed of the River Rhine, producing and working gold. Up to the beginning of the First World War, and perhaps even later, but before modern pollution, it was possible to cross the river from one side to the other and be able to see the stones at the bottom all the way across. A high percentage of these boulders were pure quartz and the cold currents were well able to move them so that one scraped over another and possibly illuminated itself in the process. Such sights must have been stunning at night and could well have given rise to all manner of local folklores.

Subconscious Mind Sometimes called unconscious mind. The part of the brain that people cannot usually access and which produces dreams.

Supernatural Anything abnormal or extraordinary, which does not fit into the usual explanations taught in schools, colleges and universities. This word has become a dumping ground for all manner of knowledge that does not fit into the normal everyday thinking. Thus it is easy to label anyone thinking about such subjects as eccentric or daft and to disregard their discoveries, even when they are supported by hard evidence.

Superstition An accepted belief, custom or irrational fear. While some superstitions come about as a result of one person wanting to impose his domination over another, a good number of superstitions are based on more practical facts. For example, not to shelter under tall isolated trees during thunderstorms because they are likely to attract lightening. People constantly faced with the natural elements tend to be more superstitious than those cuddled up in well-insulated urban environments. The most successful German U-boat of the Second World War (U48), for example, was governed through a fairly long set of well-established nautical superstitions. The crew would not put out of a homeport on Fridays and they always steered a course divisible by the lucky number seven. A good number of these superstitions formed the basis for early laws and etiquette and some of them are carried out to this day without anyone any longer knowing the reason for carrying them out.

Sword A male symbol for fire found on tarot cards and used by some covens as a substitute for the athame. However, swords do not have a place in Traditional Witchcraft ceremonies.

Symbols An emblem, abbreviation, sign, token, colour or object representing something else other than itself. The meaning of some symbols have to be learnt and are then stored in the person's mind in the same way as any other information. For example, the letters used to identify chemical elements of the periodic table. Other symbols have such deep roots in the subconscious of many people that they are automatically interpreted in a similar manner. It is highly likely that the interpretation of symbols is even more deeply ingrained than language.

Tarot Cards A set of cards similar to playing cards but often slightly larger and with either very simple of more complicated illustrations used for divination.

The illustrations can contain many symbols, which 'speak' directly to the unconscious mind. Very little is known about their origins, other than they probably came to Europe via Italy during the fourteenth century at the time of the crusades. Some people have connected them to the ancient Hebrew alphabet and linked them to the Qabalah while others have suggested they came from ancient Egypt or even from further east. A number of different designs and types have appeared. Some have deviated from the original Tarot into parallel avenues; an example of this are the so-called Angel Cards. A number of people who called on Bill Love used Tarot cards and were thus easy targets for experimentation. The astonishing point with this was that the majority were so incredibly accurate when asked about recent developments that their results were awe-inspiring. This subject is well worth looking into.

Legend has it that an imprisoned person with no other book than the Tarot, if he knew how to use it, could in a few years acquire universal knowledge, and would be able to speak on all subjects with unequalled learning and inexhaustible eloquence. It is said that the whole initiatory wisdom of Ancient Egypt was recorded in the symbols of the Tarot cards in order to preserve the wisdom for future generations. Each deck consists of seventy-eight cards. Twenty-two of these are trump cards, known as the Major Arcana and the remaining fifty-six are the Minor Arcana. (Arcana is

the plural of Arcanum meaning mystery or secret.)

Telepathy A method of communication without using the usual senses such as sound, sight, smell, or normal feeling. No one has yet explained how this might work, but there is plenty of evidence that such communication is possible and people often use it without being aware of it. Yet proving this is difficult and it is not easy to conduct meaningful experiments.

Tetragrammaton A sacred name for God considered being so holy that it is often substituted with other more common words. Some modern publicity-seeking witches have hijacked the word, probably because it is not generally known by many people and therefore ideal for those wanting to project a superior air of deep knowledge. The word does not feature in and is not displayed in Traditional Wiccan circles.

Teutonic The Teutons were the first Germanic people living in what is now Denmark from about the fourth century BC. The term Teutonic has been adapted to mean of German or North European origin. Around the times of the Crusades a holy order of Teutonic Knights was established to bring Christianity into the more remote areas along the southern shores of the Baltic. Although originally with purely religious aims, the order soon became a military force and was used in the widespread expansion of the north European region. The Teutonic Knights remained active until about 1525 when Albert of Brandenburg left the Roman Catholic Church to establish Lutheranism throughout the East Prussian region.

Thought, positive and negative The subconscious cannot calculate, reason or understand negatives. Therefore it is important (and at times essential) to express everything with positive thought avoiding words such as cannot, can't, will not, won't, do not, don't etc. In addition to this, rather than use basic facts, it helps if the positive terms are hooked onto emotions. Thus, 'I will not chew my fingernails anymore' should become 'I will enjoy watching my fingernails grow' and 'I won't smoke anymore' should be changed to 'I will enjoy becoming a non-smoker.'

Totem poles, North European *See* Will-o'-the-Wisp.

Traditional Witchcraft Witchcraft practised before Gerald Gardner published his book *Witchcraft Today* in 1954.

Tree Worship The worship of trees is a worldwide phenomenon with a history going back from early cave paintings to the modern day. Tree worship has roots in the oldest nature worship. To this day people plant trees in their gardens or decorate them at Christmas and Easter time, but despite appreciating their presence, they do not worship the actual tree itself. The scriptures tell us of early Pagans worshipping trees and even making sacrifices to oaks, but there is no hard evidence that this happened. We do know that many districts had so-called Trial Oaks, where travelling judges or official arbitrators heard evidence and adjudicated. It is quite likely that such locations were also used to execute the more obnoxious brethrens of society.

No one has ever explained satisfactorily the reason for having yew trees in churchyards, but it seems likely that these have roots going back to pre-Christian times. The yew is evergreen and therefore could symbolise everlasting life and they could have been planted in churchyards because it was said that they offer some protection against ghosts. Although not so common in this country, trees have been planted along the sides of roads to provide shade and also to mark the route. This was terribly important in moister areas where a thick ground fog at night and early morning often obscures the road while it is possible to see the sky clearly above. Large wooden posts, often with intricate carvings, were also used to mark routes through treacherous countryside, especially in areas where the exact course of the correct path varied according to local conditions. For example, one section might become so boggy that the route needed a considerable diversion through firmer ground.

There is also considerable evidence that a number of wooden circles, similar to Stonehenge were constructed throughout northern Europe and one can also find similar circles made up of living yew trees. No one has yet explained what these were used for, but it seems likely that they marked special spots where occasional happenings occurred. Perhaps where Pagan festivals were celebrated. Yet, it is also possible that the trees were planted to provide protection from the wind or to help dry out soggy ground. They are exceedingly good at doing both and are still used for these purposes to this day.

Modern research has shown trees to form part of the basic images in mankind's subconscious. The Swiss psychotherapist, Dr Max Lüscher, who developed a most fascinating colour analysis that has been translated into more than thirty languages, came to the conclusion that the green colour of trees and bushes has left two different meanings in our subconscious minds. People look up to the colour because they would like to be as great and as powerful as trees or they need green foliage to hide behind. It is quite likely that trees create all manner of subconscious stirrings in our minds. People feel invigorated from spending some time at the seaside, near rivers and lakes and in forests, even when they are not into tree hugging. The fact that forests make a direct physical impression on the environment can best be illustrated with a thermometer. On hot days the shade under trees, especially in forests, is considerably cooler than direct sunlight.

These days we are taught in schools and colleges that forests are made up of four layers: a ground layer, field layer, bush layer and tree layer. This is most strange because this leaves out the most important part of the tree below the surface of the soil. People who learned from experience, such as Viktor Schauberger and modern forest gardeners, will also contradict this image of woodland. They have identified two types of tree for most species, a sun loving and a shade tolerant variety, both with distinctly different shapes. All this suggests that there is still a lot to be learned from observing trees and forests and it is not necessary to take too much notice of the latest academic publications. Finding someone with a passion for the subject is becoming increasingly difficult these days, but such people are still around and they are well worth looking for.

Unconscious Mind Sometimes called subconscious mind. The part of the brain we cannot control easily, which creates dreams and is not available directly to the conscious ego. Magical development involves the easing of communication between the conscious and the unconscious mind.

Vikings People living in northern Europe during the eighth to eleventh centuries, who expanded their influence into southern regions and Britain. They were known to have reached America al least some two centuries before Christopher Columbus supposedly discovered the West Indies.

Visualisation Forming images in the mind without using words, useful for communicating with one's own subconscious, for dowsing and for divination. An essential ingredient for magic and spell work.

Vortex A whirling mass of liquid or gas, spiralling as it moves. It would seem that air, water and energy moves by swirling around in spirals and that such formations are capable of creating their own energy from surrounding forces to increase in size until such a time that they can no longer be supported and they collapse. Sometimes when smoke rings are formed one can see that the energy within the vortex seems to move in two directions at the same time. This is a most fascinating field for people who have the time to observe, study and think. It would seem likely that early man knew considerably more about the energy in vortexes than we do today, and used this power

A Viking boat.

Above right: Incredibly powerful vortexes seen in a river and among waves crashing onto a beach. The vortexes in the river were strong enough to suck small boats down into the depths and the brown circles in here were sucked up as huge rings of mud and sand. Note that these rise to the surface at right angles to the waves.

215

to his advantage.

Wand A ritual tool used in Witchcraft ceremonies representing the element of air. There are no hard and fast rules as to what these should look like or how they might be made, although generally they are about as long as the distance from elbow to hand.

Wassailing Saluting or hailing apple trees. This ancient fertility ritual is of Anglo-Saxon origin and was thought to increase the apple yield. The trees were, and in some parts of Britain they still are, the focus of singing and toasting from a wassail bowl containing mead or cider.

Water Water ranks as one of the most misunderstood and most abused parts of our life system. It has a large number of different functions. Early man must have formed strong connections to water, for he could not live without it and this need appears to be still seated deep in his subconscious. People enjoy being close to streams; they congregate near fountains and spend large amounts of money in buying bottled spring water for drinking. It is an essential life force on the one hand and the most destructive power on the other. To understand the natural significance of water and the different types, all with their own energy variations, it is necessary to delve into the work of the Austrian forester Viktor Schauberger, who came up with a number of elementary theories, many of which can be tested quite easily. Water plays such an important role

The remains of Well Chapel near Littlebourne in Kent stands close to a huge spring of crystal clear water rising out of the chalk. It is difficult to see where the water is coming from, despite a massive torrent passing along the stream to what was once a water cress farm.

A well at Harbledown (Canterbury) Kent, which we found by dowsing for it.

in everybody's lives and in the natural cycles that it cannot be separated from them and must form a basis of all studies into natural cycles.

Wells Apart from some wells that apparently appeared suddenly when a saint prayed, the majority of water sources must have existed since time immemorial. The Pagan goddess Brigid has always been associated with wells. Some seasonal springs dry out periodically, but can be made to produce water for longer periods by digging down to aquifers below the surface of the earth. In some cases such deep water sources can be found by dowsing or by calculated guess work and holes dug in likely places. A good number of these wells have been declared holy by the church, given names and sometimes had buildings constructed on top of them. Many now serve communities as main source of their water supply. Folklore, superstitions and other tales have been attached to them. Throwing money into wells is still considered lucky. Wells have an important role in the history of mankind.

Wheel of Fire *See* Fire Wheel.

Whip *See* Scourge

Wicca Another name for Witchcraft, the Old Religion and the Craft.

Will-o'-the-Wisp Marsh gas (methane) can ignite when it comes into contact with oxygen on the surface of bogs or shallow marshy pools. The flickering flames tend to be small and would probably not be noticed at daytime. However, at night they can look like the light from a candle and travellers caught out in the dark might be tempted to walk towards such lights, thinking there is a house. Many bogs were soggy enough to swallow both horse and rider and were likely to be fatal for a person on their own. Thus it was important to stay on marked routes. The phenomenon is called *Irrlicht*, meaning getting lost light in German, and is also known as Jack-o'-the-Lantern in England plus a variety of other local names. This forms an important part in the history of Paganism as it gave rise to a culture producing posts like totem poles, though they were called 'idols' in Europe. They were also much smaller, the majority being not much taller than a person. These were put up along both sides of paths leading through wetlands and bogs as way markers, often with a female image on one side and a male on the other. Some tracks through bogs were made from logs or large bundles of heather bound together, to float on the top of the soft ground. In flooded forests people would have used boats or pontoons to move about. These markers were important to the local inhabitants because wet or moist areas were likely to attract a serious ground fog at night and this could well last until mid-morning when the sun is powerful enough to evaporate the water droplets in the air. Early man chose to live in boggy areas because they were more difficult for attackers to reach. British Iron Age hill forts were designed using similar logic and served people living in areas without hills. Fields for cattle and crops were often some distance away on firmer ground. Therefore it was essential that the routes through treacherous terrain were marked in such a way that friends could find their way and unwanted visitors got lost. *See also* Tree Worship.

Witch Even these days the word 'witch' is charged with high emotions and taken to mean an evil, old and horrid looking woman. Storybook images of witches are still used to frighten people and they are nearly always associated with devil worship, black magic and other evil activities. In addition to this, the characteristics and the accoutrements of witches are deeply engraved on many people's minds. What is interesting is that the word features in dictionaries but not in many encyclopaedias, suggesting that it is a figment of fantasy rather reality. A witch can be male as well as female and the majority of people do not know that it refers to a person who lives in harmony with nature and tries to use natural remedies in preference to modern medicines.

Witch, Hedge Someone living the way of the witch but without being a member of a coven; a solitary practitioner.

Witch, Black A bad or evil witch. In northern folklore there are good looking evil witches to confuse the unwary.

Witch, White A good witch.

Witch-hunt This originally referred to the Inquisition when the Christians persecuted everyone not following the doctrine of the Church. These days it is also used for the persecution of any opposition or socially non-conformist groups.

Witch, the name It would seem that many people who join non-conformist ways of life also need a different name to the one they were given by their parents. People joining Wiccan covens often feel they need to adopt a witch name. This has no place in a Traditional Witchcraft coven.

Witchcraft Another word for Wicca, the Old Religion or the Craft.

Witchcraft Today A book written by Gerald Gardner and published in 1954.

Yggdrasil The mighty ash from North European folklore. This huge tree had its roots in the earth and its branches reached up to the sky or heaven where the spirits were thought to live. Ash is in many way ways stronger than oak, but being a 'sweet' wood it rots quicker and therefore is not much use in wet environments. Ash saplings will grow considerably straighter than oak and such poles make ideal handles because they are strong, but not as heavy as other 'hard' timbers.

Yule One of the lesser sabbats. In Britain this was used as an alternative for Christmas, but it refers to the mid-winter festival when the hours of daylight are at their shortest, known as the Winter Solstice, which falls on 21-22 December.

Yule log Even modern people with wood burning stoves are not always aware of the different properties of firewood. Yet, knowledge of this is essential if one lights fires inside wooden houses with thatched roofs. To make matters worse, the loft space of some early north European houses was used for storing hay, and fires vented straight into this area. (Chimneys were not invented until some time later.) Sparks would have been disastrous in such conditions, although the smoke was ideal for preserving foods and timbers. Wet or green wood was likely to produce a lot of smoke and recently felled timber can make the best sparks. This meant that the preparation of Yule logs and any other timber to be burned during the depth of winter needed the qualities of burning for a long time without producing too much smoke and as few sparks as possible. People needed heat, rather than big flames from their fires. To achieve these ideal conditions, firewood needs to be matured or seasoned for a considerable period in an airy environment before use. Many north European houses had large protruding eaves so that firewood could be stacked under them against the outside wall for seasoning. Nordic people also stacked firewood in circular piles, around a central pole and with a thatched roof resting on top of the wood that was capable of sliding up and down the pole. For Pagans the Yule log signifies the death of darkness and the new sun's heat. Some wood from the log should be saved in order to start the next year's fire. Traditionally the log should burn for twelve days with the first day being on the Winter Solstice.

FURTHER READING

Some of the books mentioned by Bill are now so exceedingly rare that it will be difficult to find them. Therefore, they have not all been included in this list.

Alexandersson, Olaf, *Living Water*, Gateway Books, Bath, 1982 (About Viktor Schauberger and the secrets of natural energy.)

Andrews, Ted, *How to See and Read the Aura*, Llewellyn Publications, St. Paul, 2001 (A small but most interesting and useful book with plenty of practical advice.)

Applegate, George, *The Complete Guide to Dowsing*, Element, Shaftsbury, 1997

Ashcroft-Nowicki, Dolores, *The Tree of Ecstasy*, The Aquarian Press, London, 1991

Chadwick, Nora, *The Celts*, Penguin Books, Harmondsworth, 1970

Coats, Callum, *Living Energies*, Gateway Books, Bath, 1996 (Viktor Schauberger's brilliant work with natural energy explained.)

Cunningham, Scott, *Living Wicca*, Llewellyn Publications, St. Paul, 1997 (A guide for the solitary practitioner. Recommended by Bill.)

Connolly, Eileen, *Tarot*, Thorsons, London, 1995 (The complete handbook for the apprentice.)

Devereux, Paul, *The New Ley Hunter's Guide*, Gothic Image, Glastonbury, 1994

Durkheim, Emily, *The Elementary Forms of the Religious Life*, George Allen & Unwin Ltd., London, 1915 & 1971

Farrar, Janet and Stewart and Bone, Gavin, *The Pagan Path*, Phoenix

Publishing, Washington, 1995 (This books helps to answer why Paganism is the fastest growing religion in the world.)

Farrar, Janet and Stewart, *Eight Sabbats for Witches*, Robert Hale, London, 1981

Farrar, Janet and Stewart, *The Witches' Way*, Robert Hale, London, 1984

Fordham, Frieda, *An Introduction to Jung's Psychology*, Penguin Books, London, 1966

Fortune, Dion, *Through the Gates of Death*, Weiser Books, Maine, 2000

Frazer, Sir James George, *The Golden Bough*, MacMillan, London, 1922 & 1963

Gardner, Gerald, *High Magic Aid*, M. Houghton, Atlantis Bookshop, London, 1949

Gardner, Gerald, *Witchcraft Today*, Rider, London, 1954

Graham, Helen, *Visualisation*, Piatkus, London, 1996

Graves, Robert, *The White Goddess*, Faber and Faber, London, 1962 & 1984

Green, Marian, *A Harvest of Festivals*, Kongmans, London and New York, 1980

Hannant, Sara, *Mummers, Maypoles and Milkmaids*, Merrell Publishing, London and New York, 2012 (A journey through the English ritual year.)

Harding, M. Ester, *Woman's Mysteries*, Rider, London, 1955

Hartley, Marie and Joan Ingilby, *Life and Traditions in the Yorkshire Dales*, J. M. Dent and Sons, 1968 and re-printed by Dalesman Books, Lancaster, 1985 (An interesting social history of what life must have been like when Bill's coven moved out of Northumberland to create a new branch in Essex.)

Hesemann, Michael, *The Cosmic Connection*, Gateway Books, Bath, 1996 (Worldwide crop formations and ET contacts. A general introduction.)

Hole, Christina, *A Dictionary of British Folk Customs*, Paladin, London, 1976 & 1984

Madders, Jane, *Stress and Relaxation*, Martin Dunitz, London, 1979 (Self help techniques for everyone.)

Malinowski, Bronislaw, *Magic, Science and Religion and other Essays*, Souvenir Press, London, 1948

Murray, Margaret, *The Witch Cult in Western Europe*, Oxford University Press, London and Oxford, 1921

Murray, Margaret, *The God of the Witches*, Oxford University Press, London and Oxford, 1931 & 1970

Neumann, Erich, *The Great Mother*, Princetown University Press, New York, 1974

Palmer, Alan, *Northern Shores*, John Murray, London, 2005 (A history of the Baltic Sea and its peoples. Most readable and interesting.)

Ross, Anne, *Pagan Celtic Britain*, Constable, London, 1992

Springett, Ulli, *Symbol Therapy*, Piatkus, London, 2001

Starhawk, *The Pagan Book of Living and Dying*, Harper One, New York, 1997

Talbot, Michael, *Mysticism and the New Physics*, Routledge & Kegan Paul, London and Henley, 1981

Valiente, Doreem, *Witchcraft for Tomorrow*, Robert Hale, London, 1985

Watson, Lyall, *Supernature*, Hodder and Stoughton, London, 1974

West, Peter, *Biorhythms*, Thorsons Publishing, Northamptonshire, 1980